BOOK ONE

# Gifts from
# Lake Cowichan

*by* Patricia Baumgardner

BOOK TWO

# Legacy from Fritz

*by* Fritz Perls

Science and Behavior Books, Inc.
Palo Alto, California

The Publisher gratefully acknowledges the permission granted by Aquarian Productions, Ltd. and Media-Psych Corporation for the use of transcripts based on their film productions as text in this book.

Aquarian Productions, Ltd.
Suite 301 Heather Medical Building
720 West Broadway
Vancouver 9, B.C.

Media-Psych Corporation
Post Office Box 7707
San Diego, California 92107

For information about rental of these films, please contact the film producers direct.

Typeset by Vera Allen Composition Service,
Castro Valley, California

Library of Congress Catalog Card Number 75-23594

ISBN 0-8314-0046-3

**BOOK ONE**

**BOOK TWO**

# Legacy from Fritz 89

## Chapter 1

### The Teachings 93

## Chapter 2

### The Therapy 117

# Foreword

The title of this volume, *Legacy from Fritz*, has a special meaning for me. In December, 1969, at a time when Fritz looked very good to me, he said that he felt he was at the peak of his writing and teaching ability. He signed a contract with Science and Behavior Books to write a book or series of books on his philosophy and practice of psychotherapy. He asked me to prepare transcriptions of the lectures he had given in the past few months at Cowichan. He felt these lectures caught the influence of Eastern thought. He also wanted transcriptions of his films. He thought that detailed study of the transcriptions could make his films the basis of exciting discovery. He also gave me a manuscript to look over and indicated he would draw ideas from it. He was to return to Cowichan and pull all of this together.

Fritz died several months later, never having returned to Lake Cowichan. The question I was faced with was what was I to do with this mass of material? I sent it off to John Stevens and Joen Fagen, but both of these talented people were too busy.

The first volume came together rather easily. With very little editing, the manuscript became *The Gestalt Approach*. The second part of the book contained transcripts of films. Incidentally, most Gestalt historians think the *Gestalt Approach* was written before Fritz's Esalen days and probably was revised very little.

The problem of what to do with the rest of the material left to me by Fritz was a formidable one. A serendipitous solution presented itself when I heard a series of talks by Patricia Baumgardner which pulled together what she had learned from Fritz during the last three months at Cowichan. Pat retained a vivid impression of her time with Fritz. His teachings became the basis of her work in the years since Fritz's death.

The rest of *Legacy from Fritz* is again edited by Richard Bandler in the same sensitive manner in which he edited *The Gestalt Approach*.

This volume completes the task that Fritz assigned to me.

Robert S. Spitzer, M.D.
Editor-in-Chief

# BOOK ONE

# Gifts from
# Lake Cowichan

*by* Patricia Baumgardner

*I give warm thanks to you my friends who work in therapy with me and have been willing to make available for my writing parts of your own special journeys in psychotherapy.*

P.B.

## Author's Note

Fritz Perls lived in the present. He moved into memories of
the past and fantasies of the future as dimensions of experience immediately present. Sometimes I write in the present
tense as through memory I hear and see Fritz now.

# To Fritz

I write almost five years after Autumn, 1969, at Lake Cowichan with you, Fritz. For me, five years of growing awareness and touching other lives in a special way was made possible in those months of living with you. At this time, I am not aware of much unfinished business from my time of being physically with you.

I want very much to tell you what I have learned since.

Your gift to me endures in my body, which is warmer and quieter, and in my feelings which flow more and more clearly. I have not given up my pride, which you first showed me face-to-face, and neither do I feel its hopeless captive. You have made possible the best ways I know for working and growing.

I feel unfinished in the matter of balance. You spent the last working months of your life training therapists; people who were to go out from your workshop center to carry to other men and women the therapy you had developed. You told us of places the world over that were asking for speakers and therapists. You asked me whether or not I would like to go and live and work in Boston.

You gave me much of yourself. You worked with me over and over and continuously—even to telling me to get up and work when I avoided it. Then, at last, one night, I put down my controlling and learning that I could survive. And I never went to Boston, or anywhere else except back home to practice quietly. I have not helped beyond my own living and working to share with others the results of your work.

So, I have lived with my passivity, and with my urgency to act, to share what I can, beyond those who happen to come to my office, of all that you have given me.

And now I am writing it down, Fritz. And it seems to have come out a personalized, partial variety of Gestalt primer. I have not written down all that I remember of my experience and learning with you; only that which has offered to me most meaning, workability, and potential. You gave and did much more. I hope that this primer, including some of my memories and experiences of you and your working, will help with the balance I mentioned earlier. I hope that people will find through reading of my experiences some access to you.

# To the Reader

The thoughts I share with you now are an integration of some of my experiences with Fritz and what has happened since and my own processing and elaborating of those experiences.

A few months ago I gathered together in my mind and then on paper some of the ideas I had brought back from my time four years ago with Fritz. These thoughts have to do with my most important discoveries about psychotherapy, as a student of Fritz at Vancouver Island and before those months when Fritz was still at Esalen, and during the years since 1969. My writing at this particular time seems arbitrary indeed, as I imagine the days and years of the future, and see myself continuing to learn from what Fritz has provided.

I wanted to put into words as best I could some varieties of experience and thinking available for the process of therapy, some ideas about how the therapist can be and what he can do, which I've discovered to be effective and basic.

Fritz's concepts and theoretical structure are well documented. I've wanted not to add to this literature but rather to share my own special learning and some of my experience in the area of acting as therapist, which I understand to be a matter of allowing my whole process to flow so that someone else who is with me will risk going a new way.

I've written of what I've found with Fritz first of all for my daughters, Christine and Anne, who work with Gestalt therapy and who live increasingly in the Gestalt way, and for a small group of friends who meet together to study, finding that Fritz is with us often.

Now I think beyond my known friends to those of you who find in Gestalt therapy a special promise and have not had the chance to know Fritz or perhaps anyone close to him. I want to share my experience, beginning with Fritz and profoundly affected by him, especially with you who feel some degree of commitment to existential therapy and who work with otherwise healthy people who are troubled or stopped in their growth toward wholeness and increasing creativity. For those people who seek to expand their own evolution there is recourse in Gestalt therapy through the discovery on a deeply experiential level that they have induced their own dilemmas and consequently hold the key themselves to recovery.

## CHAPTER ONE

# Gifts from Lake Cowichan

Gestalt therapy is a matter of attending to another human being in a way which makes it possible for him to be himself, "grounded in the power which constitutes him," to borrow a phrase from Kierkegaard.[1]

Continuing in Kierkegaard's tradition, Gestalt therapy is an existential therapy, concerned with the problems evoked by our dread of accepting responsibility for what we are and what we do.

Fritz has developed a process of therapy which, ideally or in its pure state, avoids concepts. He distinguishes "talking about" and morality from the process of therapy, leaving us to work with the data, or the observable behavior which constitutes the phenomenon, rather than with our own and the other person's hypothesizing. Gestalt therapy first differentiates and then is concerned with and utilizes what we experience rather than what we think. This means that the Gestalt therapist must provide a special situation. He becomes a catalyst who facilitates the client's awareness of what exists at this moment, and who frustrates the client's varieties of avoidance.

Fritz introduces as the basis of his own conceptualizing, the idea of "Gestalt," suggesting two specifics: complete or whole, and formation. He refers to the Gestalt as the "ultimate experiential unit." "Experience" of ourselves is largely physical, and so dependent upon awareness of our bodies. The notions of bodily needs and of unfinished situations, and their interrelations, are basic. As the need of the organism is satisfied through giving to and taking from the environment, the Gestalt is completed, the situation finished. Awareness of the need diminishes and disappears, and new awareness can emerge. The organism is open for the appearance of another unfinished situation and the energy which will come with this new demand.

The purpose of psychotherapy is to restore lost parts of the personality. Our disowned experience and functioning can be recovered. This process of taking back, re-integrating and experiencing again is the province of psychotherapy. The therapist involves himself with the client in the process of reowning sensations and behavior which he has given up and now finds alien, until the client begins to and can continue on his own to assert and act in terms of the person he really is.

We are concerned with ego boundaries, with "me" and "not me." And with how another person has long ago transformed parts of "me" and "not me." We see him now unwilling to own a sadistic wish, perhaps even an angry impulse. Maybe he prefers not to acknowledge that it is indeed he who has just come in for his appointment managing to arrive a half hour late. He states, and believes, that someone or something else owns this avoidance. The heavy traffic takes over his autonomy and makes him late, or someone else called on the telephone and delayed him. Or sometimes, a compulsion to get everything done before leaving home, his "upbringing" existing as beyond the client's control and so not belonging either to his responsible self: "I can't help it." Often what has been forbidden and given up is the experience of success or importance; sometimes any way at all of being which the person imagines might prove unacceptable to someone else.

So, as we reject and throw beyond our ego boundaries our feelings and our natural ways of being, we compress ourselves, becoming structured and artificial and showing patterns of behavior having little to do with our real selves. And, having given away selected parts of ourselves, we become separated from our energy and our power. Here Fritz takes us to the heart of the matter; there is no extensive giving up parts of ourselves, those ways of being and doing which are our very selves, without loss of vitality. As we turn away a feeling or an impulse to act, we interrupt the flowing of energy which supports our organismic being. Fritz offers a way to re-appropriate this energy which is our lost power: by finding a way to get in touch again with our alienated selves. We must be willing to allow again the forbidden awareness and to accept and integrate these feelings and behavior which have become "not me."

Gestalt therapy gives us a methodology. This way of working depends upon our differentiating "talking about" and experiencing. We are familiar with the patient who arrives for therapy after five or so years of previous treatment which consisted mostly of "talking about." He is able to recite a dissertation on his personality functioning and pathology, and he is still suffering, still defeating himself,* still, pragmatically, pretty much where he was before the five years. He knows everything and he understands little. It is not enough to "know" in the sense of being able to explain. If the client is to know his own power through therapy, so that he comes to rely on himself, to act out of his selfhood, and to cope effectively with the world without selling out what he values, we must offer him experience.

By experience, I refer to being in contact. In contact, or in touch, with oneself and with one's world, as opposed to "thinking about." I am remembering Fritz's saying to us: "If I allow the patient to stay in his head, I must know that nothing will change for him." The methodology of Gestalt therapy consists of returning again and again to a relational mode of being.

We are in the business of identifying and working with the patient's make-believe social roles and of filling up the holes in his personality. We are interested in those roles which leave the patient feeling drained and nowhere, because they are in conflict with his biological needs. The patient's experience of emptiness, his avoidances, those

---

* (I do not mean to suggest that people who enter into Gestalt therapy cannot suffer the same fate. If the full course of therapy is not fulfilled and therapy is interrupted, this return to old patterns of self-defeat is exactly what may occur.)

areas where he does not cope and where he looks to the presumed abilities of others, are indicators of his holes.

What I saw as I watched Fritz work confirmed his stated conviction about the work of therapy, that the purpose is indeed to deal with these two phenomena: phony roles and holes in the personality. Fritz then turns to point out the method, which is to attend continuously to awareness, and the major tools which the patient brings, his voice and his demands within the therapeutic situation. And so Fritz provides and elaborates all that we need: purpose, method, tools. He makes a giant contribution as he exposes interrelationships among these phenomena: social roles and holes in the personality, awareness, voice, demands. Perhaps no single gift of Fritz's has been more important to me than this, his often repeated quotes: "Maya, maya; all is play." "All is play, and only the wise few know it." These words which Fritz spoke as we worked and lived together I understand ever more fully as I experience the power of integrating the Gestalt purpose, method and tools. It is the patient's "play" which we must explore, in its expression, effect, value, and its relation to the self.

Let's take a look at two of the major theoretical statements of Gestalt therapy in relation to psychoanalytic concepts. Fritz sees neurosis as the process of becoming unaware, and progressively separated from one's potential as experience is denied. This notion corresponds to Freud's concepts of repression and inhibition, and provides the basis for Fritz's statement of the purpose of therapy, which is to reverse the behavior of repression, or making oneself unaware. Fritz introduces a critical reversal from Freudian theory, changing and significantly opening up the nature and potential of psychotherapy. He submits that Freud hypothesizes exactly backward regarding the role of early destructive experience and the self-defeating behavior which results and persists. The issue then becomes one of whether childhood trauma is, as psychoanalytic theory states, "fixating" and controlling ever after, or whether it might become with time a believable excuse. Fritz submits that we cherish and cling to the unhappy past to avoid taking responsibility for what we do and for growing up into self-sufficient

12

behavior, as opposed to Freud's notion that we remain infantile inevitably since we are helplessly controlled by events of long ago. This is an issue of transcending importance for the therapist, involving the nature of his faith at the deepest level in the potential of psychotherapy.

Gestalt theory assumes that the human organism and its environment, including other people, are a unit and not divisible. One does not occur without the other. Gestalt therapy concerns itself with what goes on between the organism and the environment on the biological and on the social levels. Body awareness is a continuous, probably the primary ongoing source of the patient's discovering of himself in relation to what is outside of himself. The healthy self exchanges in a relatively unobstructed way with the world, so that we are concerned on the biological level for example with the patient who restricts his breathing or who will not nourish his body with food; on the social-emotional level, with the person who avoids hearing or touching other people. We watch for the blocking of natural flow. When the patient has reduced or obliterated by refusing to experience large parts of his world, we find him autistic; lost in himself. We turn then to the existing process. We can begin to work immediately to discover the nature of this watching of himself, the awareness to which he denotes much of his energy, as well as to strengthen whatever he still allows of contact with his environment.

As I write of these matters which are for me the solid rock supporting the Gestalt structure, I am feeling troubled at times by words. I know of no word which is in any way adequate to refer to the person who is the subject of therapy. I do not think of people who come to work in therapy as patients or as clients. Sheldon Kopp[2] seems to come closest when he writes of the "pilgrim" of psychotherapy. Therapy, surely as we know it in the Gestalt tradition, will not succeed while we borrow indiscriminately from medical and business or educational models, observing roles and distinctions of student and teacher or the sick and the healer. If the other person brings such stereotypes, the therapist knows otherwise, and the work of two people together continues, each offering what he can. More than anything else, in the process of therapy we are seekers who look for a new way of being. As I work with someone in therapy, the word which best expresses my feeling for the person seeking, is friend. We give to each other. I write of these special friends with the customary words, patient and client, only out of knowing no better word which all of us understand together.

Fritz leaves with us:

### Gestalt:

An existential psychotherapy, which deals with what is or the existing phenomenon. Does not depend upon "talking about," or what "should be."

### Purpose:

To recover lost parts of the personality.

### Phenomena to Work With:

*Social roles.* Behavior which opposes natural process.
*Holes in the Personality.* Parts of the self which are no longer experienced or are denied expression.

### Method:

Attend continuously to awareness.

### Tools:

*For roles:* the voice.
*For holes:* avoidance; demands made by the patient in the therapeutic situation.

### The Emerging Gestalt:

One phenomenon exists at a time. Unfinished situations reveal themselves through the flow of background material into foreground figure.

### Experience:

is contact. We are in touch with ourselves through our bodies and our emotions. We experience the world with our five senses.

### Bodily Awareness:

is the key to discovering the patient's difficulties. Unfinished situations and unexpressed feelings are revealed through bodily tensions.

14

## Awareness

The basic point of departure is that only one phenomenon can be foreground at a time. If we accept this basic assumption, our energy can be directed toward being with the patient quite simply, by asking within ourselves, "What is going on?" We are rescued from the possibility of our own scrambling around, chasing innuendos, imposing our own priorities, and whatever other varieties of unrewarding efforts. We have only to discover the process occurring at this moment which is foreground for the patient.

This process of discovery proceeds through awareness. Our own and his. I'd like to consider now a few aspects of this inexhaustible subject, those which I've discovered to be necessary points of focus in the whole complex of therapy:

- Implications of the subjective character of awareness
- The awareness continuum as a means of distinguishing oneself, the world and the intermediate zone
- Awareness as the road to understanding the "how" of behavior
- Contact and withdrawal
- Emotions and muscles

Awareness is subjective. We are aware of ourselves through our bodies and our emotions. We are aware of the world as we perceive what is outside of our skin, using our senses of seeing, hearing, touching, tasting, smelling. I cannot be aware of your awareness; I know only your observable behavior. I know about you only what you are willing to let me know. This is a limitation of immense importance for psychotherapy. Again I am hearing Fritz saying: "You never know more than the person in the hot seat." I would remind myself, "I never know so much as the person in the hot seat." I perceive only the parts of you which you disclose to my senses of perception. I rely on you to let me know of your inner experiencing of your body and emotions, and the flow and change of you as events within you emerge to become foreground and then in turn recede into background.

We are speaking now of the other person's *self*-awareness, which is our means of using the "how" of events to understand his constant state of becoming. How does he feel his own continuous inner changing? If the patient is willing to state aloud his bodily and emotional awareness, omitting for the moment any thoughts, he discovers in time a series of tensions occuring which pertain to his unfinished situations. The patient expresses "discomfort." And any discomfort not induced by disease or trauma is indicative of and the result of unexpressed feeling. Our bodies signal our unwillingness to be what we really are. Through his revealing that his arms are tightened or his heart pounding, the patient puts us in touch with the "how" of his distorting himself and standing in his own way of being what he is, and this awareness of "how" is the first step along his path toward becoming himself. At the same time, as we attend to the patient's awareness of how he experiences himself, we fulfill the Gestalt requirement of working in the present. Fritz states that being present now is a matter of bringing together our attention and awareness. The Gestalt therapist continuously seeks ways to be in touch with the "how" of events occuring in the present. He attends to the flow of the patient's awareness.

Basic to this task is the differentiation of the two parts of the totality or unit which is in reality indivisible, the human being and his world. We clarify the nature and functioning of each of the two components of the whole by abstracting each in turn in our work. For we have a goal to meet early in the ongoing process of therapy; to insure that the patient grows to know when he experiences himself, when he perceives his world, and when he uses his intellect. Opening the way for the patient to make this discrimination is in my opinion basic to all else. He simply cannot work further or grow beyond, until he knows something of how to determine what is himself and what is not him but rather otherness or his environment, and until he can discover the difference between what exists and what he creates in his head; his fantasy. I work generally with people who are notably bright and articulate, and still I've met no one who comes in asking for therapy who has had less than a good deal to learn in the

matter of discriminating what is himself, his head, his world.
Once he begins to learn, he knows already, joyously, something of how much more he can do for himself than he
suspected.

So we work with basic awareness: of the self, experienced physically and emotionally, and of the world, experienced through seeing, hearing, touching, tasting and smelling. The third state of being, the intellect, Fritz refers to as
the intermediate zone, the DMZ. He is suggesting that
thinking ("spinning your computer") is not experiencing.
And he adds his contention that the intellect, this DMZ, is
the "whore of intelligence," since the total personality is
conceived as a source of intelligence. Fritz makes clear his
priorities regarding our avenues of access to information. We
discover what is happening, and how, out there in the world
or within ourselves where the event occurs, not in our heads
where it does occur. We learn from the data, not from our
own inventing and hypothesizing. This is not to minimize
intellectual functioning per se, but only as it is used to rob us
of our other powers of knowing. Freud's discovery of the
middle zone between the self and the world and of its special
significance as a stage for rehearsal is for Fritz perhaps
Freud's landmark contribution. He applauds Freud for understanding that thinking is largely rehearsing. Fritz is
concerned with specific functions of the intellect—to think,
compute, plan, remember, anticipate, fantasize, and especially to rehearse. We rehearse the future in order to avoid
living the future. We obscure the other person by placing
between ourselves and him the creations of our imaginations. Fritz goes on to show us our intellectual process as it
functions in neurosis, to produce stereotypes, prejudices,
and catastrophic expectations. To the extent that we involve
ourselves with these productions, we cannot see and hear
other people and events as they really are. In therapy, we are
critically involved with intellectual process as the form of
existence which precludes experiencing ourselves and prevents our seeing and hearing the world. Early in therapy,
hopefully, the patient discovers how he uses his head to
block experience and perception. Fritz said at Lake
Cowichan that his own level of perceptiveness, so amazing a

phenomenon to the rest of us, was only a matter of a relatively less cluttered middle zone.

We want to begin by facilitating the patient's knowing when he is in contact and when he is withdrawn; and when he experiences and when he is in his head. The basic method is the awareness continuum. Basic not only to introducing the patient to working, but to his continuing growth throughout the course of therapy and after therapy ends. During three months of watching Fritz work each day, I was struck by his returning, again and again, to use the awareness continuum. And with extraordinary results. I am remembering one particular evening now. Fritz works with me in a small group, using the awareness continuum as he asks me to see each person one by one, and express what I feel as I go along. What I feel is a great deal—annoyance, sorrow, joy and caring in turn as I see for a moment or so each familiar face. Fritz watches and listens, saying nothing as I see each person and allow my feelings to happen as they will. He gets the message of emotion welling up, intensifying, and he comments as I finish, "You see the power of this method." My feelings then and even now in memory supply the answer.

To work with the awareness continuum, ask the patient to state aloud his awareness of himself, continuing for a few consecutive moments to share only his experience of himself; then ask him to switch to stating his awareness of what is outside of him. Have him alternate, going back and forth between himself and the world. Interrupt him when he includes his thoughts, giving him an opportunity to hear himself and discover that he has left his feelings and perceptions, and now goes to his middle zone. In the workshop or group, ask him to be with himself, then with other people one at a time, returning after each one to see how he experiences himself after perceiving the other person.

When the patient has learned to share his awareness of his body and emotions as it flows, have him deliberately add his fantasy, so that he moves from perceiving the world, through his fantasy of the world and especially the other person, to his inner experience. "I see your body turned away and still, and your face frowning. I imagine that you're angry. I feel anxious." He now moves through the three ways of being, hearing himself state aloud the process which gets him into trouble as he uses his intellect to produce fantasy, which in turn sets up conditions for self torture and anxiety. He can discover by comparing his perception and his fantasy that they are different, and that his selection of the one to which he will respond matters enormously.

In the beginning, before the patient has distinguished his eyes and ears from his head and himself from the world, he tells you that he "sees" sadness, he "senses" failure, he "knows" somebody is going to blame him. He submits as established fact the varieties of his imaginings, undisturbed by any idea that he is in touch only with his own thinking and remains largely ignorant of the events occurring outside of himself. Being with people at the beginning of therapy, (and with people, including almost all of us anywhere) I find easy to believe Fritz's notion that something above ninety percent of what goes on is projection.

The awareness continuum is the foundation. Use it frequently. Have the patient share his experience as he moves from contact to withdrawal; as he moves between himself and you, between himself and others, people who are physically present and those he imagines in the empty chair. As he works with the whole spectrum of his awareness, he achieves a complex of rewards: he is involved with his senses rather than more or less exclusively with his mind, with experiencing rather than avoiding; he is in touch with the only certain knowing of himself; he learns the basic skill necessary for communication. I have found it necessary to work patiently, occasionally through my own boredom, introducing and re-introducing the awareness continuum. It takes time for people to learn to be involved and to discriminate between experience and intellectualization, between what is oneself and what is the other person. It has been my experience that until he reaches this point, the patient is simply unable to make use of all the rest that Gestalt therapy offers. Once he masters the awareness continuum, he knows how to work. He has achieved a basis for being responsible for himself and for letting be, for continuous discovering, and for communication.

Fritz says: "Rely always on the emerging Gestalt." He submits that if we are willing to wait when the patient seems to experience little and produce nothing, something will emerge with time. We wait, at such moments, believing that an internal flow of events is the natural human state, that each of us is at any time "unfinished" or unresolved emotionally, and that the nature of our emotional flowing is to allow into awareness what is unfinished.

At this point it seems important to me to distinguish between the patient who waits quietly for emergence of a significant foreground experience, and the person who is immobilized by an impasse. Is the patient emotionally alive and at peace, or does he make himself feel dead in order to avoid? Does he appear to be unaware of himself while showing us agitation? When the patient fails to indicate awareness of what to us is obvious and a clear phenomenon, we can do better than to wait. We can share our perception. "Are you aware of what your hand is doing?" He becomes aware, allows his attention to be where his energy is so that his hand can give its message, opening the way for the work of resolving the unfinished. Later on we will confront the problems of impasse and what the therapist can do. For now I am concerned with our perceiving the patient clearly enough to know whether we are in the presence of someone who allows the process of his own flow or of someone who stops himself. In general, we know then whether to wait or whether to offer the patient something of our own experience and perception.

I want to consider specifically the sequence of contact and withdrawal. Contact refers to being in touch through perception with someone or something outside of oneself, withdrawal to being isolated from the world while in touch with inner feelings or occupied with DMZ functioning. As we observe the other person, we want to know from moment to moment whether he is autistically or relationally involved. What is the quality of his rhythm as he comes and goes? What sort of contact does he allow? Where is he most of the time? After perceiving other people does he return to his feelings or to his head? At Lake Cowichan, Fritz made a point of sharing with us his understanding of people showing a high degree of autistic rather than relational behavior. These people, he stated, "have no eyes." They project themselves into the world, attempting to secure and become a focal point for attention. Instead of eyes for seeing the world, they have mirrors for getting back from other people reflections of themselves. Some people who have largely relinquished their eyes for self-images seem to resist any contact which is more than momentary, tending to retreat into detachment or anxiety when they are interrupted. The phenomenon is one of their focusing on themselves and involves also getting others to see and acknowledge them. Sometimes people even call this preoccupation "being aware." It is then important to ask repeatedly: "To whom are you saying this?" "Who do you want to be with?" "Is there someone you'd like to express this to?" Discover whether the patient is at all willing to let someone else in. And working through the awareness continuum helps to strengthen whatever eyes and ears remain. Whatever the nature of his presenting problem, the patient is trapped to some extent in focusing on himself. Therapy is necessarily concerned with this inevitable aspect of neurotic process. We begin by facilitating the patient's recognition of his commitment to focusing on himself. He can learn through becoming aware of his characteristic sequence of contact and withdrawal.

Watch the patient's withdrawing to find out what he avoids. If he feels unable to cope with what goes on around him here and now, he may go away in fantasy to a place where he feels at least more comfortable. Pay attention to what is going on in the patient's world at the time of his emotionally leaving. He may well keep himself unaware of what it is that he will not confront. The therapist must know, if he is to work with the patient's feelings of helplessness. One possibility is to ask him, when you see him struggling and stuck or beginning to avoid, to close his eyes and go away in fantasy as he wishes. After he returns, compare the place to which he goes in fantasy with the situation here and now. Compare what he feels here and what he feels there, and what is being avoided becomes apparent. He avoids a particular present situation which involves for him a particular feeling response. Sometimes it is necessary to ask the patient to go back and forth several times between here and his place of withdrawal before he gives up being stuck and running away and is willing to risk involvement. I am remembering a woman with Fritz who began to avoid as she faced her catastrophic fantasies involved in experiencing closeness. She seemed to fade away, laughing and sounding unbelievable. She went away in fantasy when he asked her to, to a sailboat. The present situation, the big brightly lit room in the meeting house where the whole group gathered for evening work, was for her ". . . bright lights, harsh, stiff, and close." There, on the sailboat, she found comfort to bring back to the here and now with its lights and people.

Sometimes Fritz asked people quite deliberately to take specific things back and forth between the real world and the place of retreat. An experience born in one place can be taken to the other, and what one feels transfers from the present situation to the fantasy world as well as the other way around. A feeling, a gesture, a gift given here can be taken to the fantasy place to finish emotionally an event which is past. Fritz worked with me one morning close to the end of our time on Vancouver Island, as I went back again to a time of some years ago which I hadn't finished, the day of my husband's death. Fritz told me to take my love for him, for Fritz, back to my husband. I did what he asked, and felt peaceful again, able to let go of some grief from long ago.

Two additional points I find important, one regarding contact and one having to do with vitality. Contact contains an aspect of its opposite—isolation. I am seeing Fritz looking evenly at us, one after another, and saying slowly: "Contact is the appreciation of differences." I believe that he refers to contrast, that perception of differences which must exist if we are to experience otherness. I can be with you only as I am certain that you are "not-me"; that we exist as separate entities from each other. Fritz goes on to point out that without the separation ingredient in contact, we have not contact, but confluence. Now we have no longer two distinguishable beings in relation to each other. We perceive instead a "flowing with," or moving as one, the confluence which occurs when one person gives up his separateness in relation to another.

Recognize which of the two phenomena occurs—contact or confluence. The person who experiences real contact cooperates; without contact, he complies. In the first instance, the patient continues to experience himself as separate from the therapist while remaining in touch and involved. He responds at least to some recognizable degree by knowing what he feels and acting on it. He himself emerges. In the event of confluence, the patient merely complies. He submits. On the surface he appears to hear and to respond, to be "relevant" and wanting to go along. If we listen and look, we find the deadness of compliance. The patient offers nothing vital out of his own uniqueness; he has given up his difference. As long as the patient merely flows along with the therapist, nothing happens for him. We must first recognize that we are in the presence of confluence and work with this phenomenon as the happening which is foreground.

Contact is then a condition of the therapeutic process. This would appear to be a simple fact, since contact, or experience, is the essential ingredient in growth and in life itself. We find in therapy if not before that the fact is not so simple, that real contact is elusive.

How then does contact come about? Fritz shared some thoughts at different times: "We cannot make contact. Contact is. We touch each other by being what we honestly are." People talk of "trying" to be in touch. They have not understood that contact can only be allowed, never produced on demand. Time and work are necessary for most of us to begin to know that all we can do is to get out of our own way so that contact can occur. As we work with the awareness continuum, the client begins to experience what it means to let be. He can take the next step only then, the step of discovering that when he lets go of his efforts to control and allows contact to happen if it will, his own power and vitality emerge anew. We are back to awareness. And Fritz's voice comes back to me saying, "Awareness is everything."

The quality of vitality is an expression of the sequential functioning of both kinds of contact, with oneself and with the world. Fritz emphasizes how the one experience is vitalized by the other. Let's look at some significant pragmatic implications. If the patient won't see or hear, maybe he will get in touch with himself. Or if he refuses to know what he feels, is he willing to perceive his environment at all? Either way, the other process can then be strengthened as well. Consider, for example, the problem of anxiety, that most ubiquitous of obstructions. Asking the patient to leave his symptoms for a long enough time to hear and see even a bit of what is around him can be an effective means of getting beyond the barrier of anxiety to what he feels and blocks from his awareness. If the patient experiences anxiety, he indicates that he has lost contact with himself and is unwilling to know what he really feels. Ask him to share with you what he gets in touch with outside of himself. After he tells you what he sees and hears and he returns again to himself, often he will feel quieter, his feelings distinguishable, and better able to begin to move. I am remembering a bright, able young woman who produced symptoms of anxiety at critical moments of her existence and so insured each time that once more she would fail. After confining herself to her house for three years, she began therapy and secured a job. She reports arriving at the scene of her work feeling acute anxiety. We discover that she is seeing and hearing almost nothing. I tell her to go back again in fantasy to her job situation, where I ask her for more and more of what she sees and hears. She shuttles back and forth between her feelings and the scene of her working, finding ever more to perceive, and we discover as she returns to herself intermittently that her anxiety lessens and feelings of anger emerge. Her emotions have been enhanced by her contact with the world until her anger emerges above the threshold of her awareness, and anxiety gives way to vital feeling.

Emotions, in turn, are oneself, our basic energy and motivators of behavior. Feelings stimulate bodily movement. We work from the basic assumption that Fritz observed often: emotions have muscular components. We have grounds for wondering about the patient who appears continuously still and quiet. When natural process is allowed, inner experience or emotion occurs and mobilizes muscles, leading to observable behavior. This movement becomes part of the experience of others and leads to taking from the world, and we see the reciprocal process which Fritz has called "exchanging with the world." When the patient remains consistently quiet, prohibiting movement, his energizing process is disturbed and his involvement diminished. We must then find ways of facilitating his allowing his body to move again.

Gestalt therapy teaches us about and features the importance of body awareness. With this new dimension, basic and paramount, comes a methodology for discovering feelings which are held beyond awareness. We are concerned with the "how" of the patient's tying up his body. We look to whatever awareness he has of his body. His discovering muscle tensions, together with his learning to allow his body to take over and to send its messages—his letting be—opens the way for change to occur. With awareness of tension, the body held rigid can begin to move, the unconstricted body opens, and the patient's feelings begins to flow again. At times of seeing such flowing change, I feel awe, as I might feel in the presence of a miracle. And I hear again Fritz's promise: "Awareness per se—by and of itself—can be curative."[3] A critical transformation, realizable through nothing else I know of, emerges naturally, born of simple awareness.

Again the relationship of emotion and body appears in a distinctive form, in our left-right split. Fritz sees the left side of our bodies as expressive of the sensoric or feeling system, the right side of our bodies as motoric, coping process. Or of the Yang and the Yin, our masculine and feminine beings. I have seen the relationship borne out many times, often in dreams. To get through the place where the patient is stuck when his flow of feeling into motoric behavior is blocked, have him become aware of one side and then of the other. Then ask him to have a dialogue between his right and left sides, or perhaps between parts of each side which happen to be foreground. Usually dramatic contrast emerges as the patient experiences himself alternately as his two sides. As he becomes each one side in touch with the other, expression of bodily awareness leads easily to feelings of frustration and demands, passivity, and assertion. Polarities can emerge, emotion enters the exchange, and some integration begins.

# A Place for Therapy

"I cannot help you to do it, but I can provide a place where you can do it."

Fritz's words, spoken at Esalen before he left to begin his community at Lake Cowichan on Vancouver Island. We are at lunch, side by side at a long table now almost empty. Fortunately for me, this is a meal when Fritz is not observing silence. I am asking him about his proposed place for residential training which is now soon to come into being, and I'm sharing with him how I feel stuck and unfinished. Maybe he can help me. He clears that up quickly. "I cannot help you to do it . . . ." And, Fritz-like, he gives me a gift packaged in a few words, to become ever memorable. "I can provide a place. . . ." We arrange for my going up for a visit. And now, seeing his place another way, Fritz is telling me how Lake Cowichan is like a little bit of Switzerland.

The work of the therapist is to provide a place—a special place where someone else can discover how to relate to himself, and to will to be himself. We can provide this special place by attending to the patient in a particular way. The "way" evolves as we stay in the present situation, concerning ourselves with the "how" of behavior. To the extent that we succeed in creating a place to discover and experience how it is that events occur at this moment of our being together, the patient has available the best that we can contribute to the work he has come to do. Commitment to working with the flow of existing phenomena rests upon two basic assumptions of Gestalt therapy; only the present moment exists, and what the patient does now, he does also in his existence outside the therapeutic situation. Being with someone now means attending to whatever awareness he brings, and to awareness of the process of ourselves as well—Fritz's notion of combining attention and awareness. The continuously emerging Gestalt, or flow of events within the patient from background into foreground, reveals to us the "how."

We are imagining a way of attending. Let's look for a moment at the therapist, at his body, his feelings, and what he is about, as he prepares to go to work. The therapist is simply available. He uses his ears and his eyes to perceive the obvious. He hears and sees, hopefully, whatever exists to perceive, the phenomenon another human being creates. In response, the therapist is what he is. He allows himself to respond internally as he will, being in touch with his body and his feelings. Playing therapist to me means observing a selective economy of expression of my response. I want ideally to stay in relatively close touch with my feelings, my body, my voice, to know a lot about how I feel and change inside. I want to express outwardly only that part of my inner experience which I believe has a reasonable chance of facilitating the work of therapy. Along with this process of selective response, I want to give no false messages. I hope to know at least something of what I am at a given moment, to let be, and to convey nothing to the contrary. For if I pretend or become unreal, try to hide or mislead, I act to block the client's authenticity as well. He is left without someone who can be with and available to him. With an exception which we will get to later, a special way of attending includes being oneself. I am hearing Fritz's voice. His voice is soft, and I am feeling touched and sad and caring. "I will be with you. I will be with you, with my interest, my boredom, my patience, my anger, my caring. I will be with you."

The hidden assumption is that the other person offers something with which to be. If, on the other hand, he produces nothing, we can then withdraw, perhaps to a place of our own or to rest. We can experience our own rhythm of contact and withdrawal. Don't try to stay with nothing. Fritz points out, and I find his distinction useful indeed, the difference between using energy to attend deliberately, a heavy task and exhausting, and using our awareness, which is an ongoing condition of being. If we demand of ourselves that we stay with the other person consistently, we begin to make an implicit demand of him rather than to be available for what he offers. We've ruled out and we fight against our own natural coming and going; we are no longer centered. Awareness is. We can allow it; we cannot mobilize it.

I am talking now about the notion, "let be." Fritz's injunction: "Don't push the river; it flows by itself." Let him be; let me be. Only then do we allow what exists to become evident. Simply to allow our natural flow and to be with what comes along offers to the patient the process which is opposite to inventing possibilities in the DMZ and then hassling—the procedure involved in neurotic behavior.

"Letting be" and "being with" are incompatible as well with assuming the role of the helper. If I am the helper, then you are the one being helped. I have therefore some power which you do not have—exactly the status quo which the client presents to us and urges on us. In the event of our playing the helper, he finds us stuck ourselves at the point where he came in. If we get sucked into his game, believing that out of our greater power we can "help," we can only go 'round and 'round with the patient, assuring that he remains where he now pretends to be, relatively helpless, still asking us to show the way. The Gestalt position in the matter of so-called "helping" is clear: "I take full responsibility for myself: I take no responsibility for you." Fritz makes an equation: "Taking responsibility for someone else, interfering with his life, and feeling omnipotent, are all the same." I am remembering Fritz's great gift one evening when I asked for what he could not provide, "You can count on my love, and not on my support."

In the place we make for the work of therapy through our way of attending, we sent to another human being an implicit message: "I cannot help you. I will be with you. You will do what you find necessary."

# Behavior To Recognize: Related Gestalt Implications

First, let's outline the theoretical background which Fritz provides for observing the patient through the course of therapy. For the Gestalt therapist, specific behavior is to be perceived and understood within the context of these ideas. Fritz's theoretical formulations, including his setting forth "layers of neurosis," are clear and explicit. He provides a generalized map of the journey through therapy. The therapist must recognize the point on the map which the patient-traveler has reached, if he is to know how to respond. Vastly different therapist participation is indicated at the successive stages along the way, even though superficially the patient may look and sound at a given moment as he did at an earlier point. If you have your map in hand, the patient will let you know where he is, whatever the overlay of similarities and no matter how unique his journey.

Becoming neurotic is becoming unaware. A process of progressive giving up of experience begins. As a human being allows himself less and less of the perception and response of which he is capable, as he puts out of reach his immediate "knowing" of his world and himself, two distinct phenomena occur: deadness of his spirit and vitality and holes in his personality. Deadness we hear and see; the patient's missing parts or holes we must infer.

Looking more closely at what happens to us as we become neurotic, we come to the first stage of our denying what we really are, when our excitation or feelings are blocked from flowing into motoric behavior. We experience then the discomfort of powerful emotions withheld from expression. Resolution of this turmoil and pain can be attained if we proceed to a next step: we can minimize or do away with the uncomfortable excitation by diminishing or eliminating emotions. Blocked then not only from being but even from knowing ourselves, we become anxious and inevitably begin to pretend, or to place roles. Since we can no longer cope with the world and get what we want directly, we must find another way. And since we have lost much of our own power with the giving up of so much self, we now attempt to manipulate others to provide what we seem to lack. Now Fritz's words come back: "Always, playing phony roles and manipulating the world for support are identical."

I want to review Fritz's five layers of neurosis, with a descriptive word or so. Here is the stripped-down essence of the roadmap he has left us. Consider it, so that we can understand together our general course for the individual journey of evolution through therapy.

*The Cliche*—Meaningless formalities.

*Role Playing*—Behaving "as if." Our Existence.

*Impasse*—Existence blocked or given up. Feelings of whirling, panic, being lost.

*Implosion*—Feelings contracted. Fear of nothingness and death.

*Explosion*—Resolution of opposing equal forces of implosion through spontaneous feeling.

*Life*—Feelings of trust. Positive assertion of creativity.

The work of the therapist lies largely in layer or area two, in identifying and working with roles, filling up the holes in the personality, and clarifying the client's existential dilemma. When the client no longer plays his "as if" roles, he strikes an impasse where he experiences having no way to go, behind which we find anxiety relating simply to being what he is. He resolves his anxious feelings by making himself feel and act dead. At this, the implosive level, his energy is unavailable to him. Through explosion into feeling, energy is released, and authentic life occurs. Gestalt theory asserts that the person who is most fully alive must be able to have four kinds of explosions, into joy, anger, sex, and grief.

Let's consider briefly now some common general kinds of behavior which are of importance in fulfilling the course of therapy, along with the Gestalt ideas which I find basic. Later on I will elaborate a bit more as we consider specifically the work of the therapist. I have in mind the dimension of involvement, avoidance, anxiety, resentment and guilt, projection, pride, self-torture, the "poisonous personality" and bear trapping.

Fritz instructs us to be aware, first of all, of the quality of the patient's involvement. The "how" of his behavior begins with the autistic-relational dimension. Clarify the issue of his involvement preference in terms of himself, his environment, or his intellect. Where is he? To who or what is he attending? If he seems not to be with you, then what *is* he in touch with? If he is with himself, what part of him, and how? If we know where the patient is, we can be with him. We can take note of his characteristic modes of involvement, and how he uses them. We see when he shifts, comes and goes, what happens in his world when he prefers to leave the present, and how he is willing to return. We learn something of how he copes within the three ways of being and how he avoids.

If the patient is regressed or withdrawn to a fantasy place and later tells us of this place, we discover the conditions he establishes to find comfort and take care of himself, and, through learning what it is that he creates there in his own preferred place, we find out what he avoids or what is missing for him in the present situation. I think of a young woman who leaves the therapy situation to go in fantasy to her bedroom where she plays her guitar and is alone. She enjoys the music she can create herself. She feels content, in touch with her own creativity, and, "No one is telling me to do something." We discover that she avoids contact which she imagines will demand of her or take from her and to which she will respond by feeling anxious, resentful, incompetent. We find then that she experiences her very self impinged upon and shrinking in relation to other people who make demands. She has given up most of her own assertive power. Now we have learned what our work requires: her special way of being composed of fantasy of a powerful intrusive world which diminishes her, and her own role of the helpless victim: the composition of her existence.

The client's avoidance speaks to us of that aspect of his world which he will not experience, reveals how he distorts and constricts himself, and provides clues to the holes in his personality. By working with his avoidance, we can open up an opportunity for the client first to become aware of his own running away, and then to risk the forbidden experience instead, if he is willing. Avoidance occurs when we leave the here and now; the present situation. Among many other avenues of escape, we can leave physically—leave by disen-gaging our eyes and ears and so shutting out the world, by deadening our response to what we do perceive, by going off to our heads. In the last event we manage to get away from both ourselves and the world. If the client finds his way out of the present continuously so that he escapes any new experience, he assures that nothing will change for him through therapy. He will continue to repeat the patterns of his existence and of relatively minimal living which his avoidance now permits.

We are concerned, therefore, with how the patient interrupts the flow of himself and of our being together; with how he avoids letting be. Out of the perhaps inexhaustible list of possibilities, let's underscore some common avoiding behavior to recognize: the patient "broadcasts," he gossips, remembers the past and imagines the future. He also uses his body, his voice, and some specific words to leave the now.

"Broadcasting" is Fritz's analogy for "talking at," or announcing one's feelings to no one in particular. Words are produced and tumble out and succeed one another, while one neither hears nor sees. I am remembering Fritz working with a woman who used broadcasting to avoid contact. I learned that day through what she and Fritz did together that if we are unaware that we are not in touch with anyone, we can broadcast and call this process being emotionally honest. Gossiping leaves the now to think about absent people. Thinking and talking about someone not present provides isolated refuge in the intellect, away from both the person at issue and the present environment. Avoidance into the past and the future is the blocking of contact through remembering and rehearsing, and again the DMZ wins the day. We can work with the past and with the future only as the patient is willing to incorporate past and future into his experiencing of the now. We can travel with our emotional beings to the past and to the future, so that they become the present. When the patient uses the past and future to avoid, on the other hand, he does not experience in the sense of becoming. He exercises his intellect as he remembers and thinks and talks about. He has left.

The patient uses his voice to leave the now: he mumbles, starts and stops, whispers and becomes inaudible, runs his words together and gets unintelligible, makes his voice an instrument for playing roles rather than for expressing what he feels. He avoids with his face and body as he turns away, looks at the floor, picks at his fingers, smiles at nothing, curls up and closes into himself, tightens his muscles. These common, familiar behavioral expressions become not so pedestrian seen as a signal of distress significant enough to call for diverting one's energy into running away.

Hear the patient make himself and the other person into things by replacing the words "I" and "you" with "it." I spend an impressive amount of time interrupting and asking people to substitute the personal pronouns for their "its" and their "things." I ask that they own parts of themselves again by changing, "Things are going badly" into "I am going badly," and "It's a sad day" into "I feel sad today." I ask that the patient reclaim a part of himself from the vast depersonalized "not me" of "it" and "things." "You" and "I" are at least potentially active, while "it" remains passive and done to. Victims experience, "it happens." We gain detachment at the cost of autonomy. Fritz points out that to make part of oneself an "it" both kills and removes that part. With one stroke the patient manages to do away with his feeling of contact and to put that contact beyond the boundary of his responsibility and control.

Fritz talks about anxiety, resentment, and guilt with special comments which are important in the fabric of Gestalt therapy. Anxiety is seen as stage fright. We imagine ourselves to be performing in that we produce some variety of behavior which is observable to others. We rehearse our performance, imagine that it does not meet the standards demanded by our pride, and torture ourselves with the physical discomfort which we call anxiety. Anxiety is an indicator that we have left the present for an imaginary trip into the future. To be anxious is by definition to be involved with fantasy and with the future. Come back to the present moment, begin to hear and see, and anxiety diminishes and disappears. Withholding and anxiety are associated. Here, it seems to me, is the key point for the therapist. Anxiety is a "substitute" emotion, occuring when we want to express or perform and will not allow ourselves to reveal what is going on inside. Powerful inner excitation must be allowed to flow into some form of expressive behavior, or anxiety inevitably results.

Resentment presents the classic case of our unwillingness either to say it or let it go. Fritz says it aptly, "the hanging-on bite." And resentment comes with a sleeper —the demand which it conceals. To resent is to be stuck, stuck with the demand we hide in order to maintain our position. We prefer to nurture our anger and evade either possible resolution. We prefer to maintain an unfinished situation and to make the other person pay. Resentment suggests, "He owes me," and guilt reverses the balance, implying, "I owe him." Fritz points out that guilt is projected resentment. For resolution of feelings of guilt, work with the patient to discover the resentment at the heart of his guilt. To work through being stuck and toward letting go of an unrewarding effort, ask the patient to express first his resentments and then his demands, and finally to take responsibility for his own demands.

Repeatedly Fritz asserts that over 90% of behavior is projection. I believe him. The matter of what is me and what is not me gets confused. We are unwilling to own parts of ourselves and prefer to perceive these parts somewhere outside of ourselves and belonging to others. Disowning occurs as a way of avoiding awareness, and the price we pay for our resulting incompleteness is loss of creative potential. Fritz makes a simple equation which becomes a crucial theoretical tenet with far-reaching implications. To give away part of oneself is to let go of some of one's power. The relevant basic assumption of Gestalt theory is that much of our lost potential can be reclaimed. For the Gestalt therapist, to observe projection is to know the work of re-experiencing which will be necessary for the client to restore alienated feelings and to enhance his power.

Two more items of behavior with special Gestalt reference are pride and self-torture. Be alert when the patient feels proud, or begins to play his pride, especially in relation to one of his favorite social roles. I am returning to one evening at Lake Cowichan when the whole group is gathered in the big room for a working session. I have worked with Fritz, and he has let me know that I am playing the good girl with him. Fritz makes the point at the ending. "You are a good mother, a good daughter, a good grand-daughter." As I walk away from the hot seat, I hear Fritz's voice from behind me, "It is extremely difficult to change behavior when the patient feels proud of that behavior." I am instantly anxious; I know that he is right. And now my anxiety melts as feelings of shame emerge, and these feelings give way in turn to wonder that I could so utterly blind myself to my pride. Since that time, as I see other people split to become in part their pride, and as I see this pride support destructive roles, I often stop immediately to work a bit with pride. I am remembering that Fritz kept handy Nietzsche's story of the argument between memory and pride and memory's quick submission as pride asserts, "It couldn't have been like that."

The phenomenon of self-torture seems to me to offer an unending study in variations. We put obstacles in our own way, suffer imagined wrongs and terrors; threaten ourselves. We produce anxiety, immobilize ourselves in conflict and indecision, cherish our favorite psychic pain-producing fantasies. We invoke images of others and seek out bits of reality to confirm our desolation. If we are among the more determined of self-frustrators, we produce nightmares. In unnumbered ways, we become our own devils, employing our energy in the service of our roles of torturer and the tortured. The devil emerges and becomes evident through our flow of energy into standing in our own way. His companion, the tortured, appears in ultimate suffering immobility. We see much thrashing about, and nothing happens. The phenomena are frustration and punishment, for the torturer and those around him. The Gestalt therapist focuses on the process and on the role. He avoids getting caught up in the issues so that he is free to identify the phenomenon as self-torture.

A final consideration of specific behavior concerns the people whom Fritz called "poisonous." Not one for finding euphemisms, Fritz defines the "poisonous personality," the person who characteristically pretends emotions which he does not feel, and whose pay-off is defeating other people. Fritz distinguishes patients showing good will enough to cooperate with the therapist, and willing at least to work and to be what they are to the degree that allows some change to occur, from those who want only to suck the therapist in, then sabotage, frustrate, invalidate him. Any behavior which assures the defeat of the therapist's objectives will do. These people are committed first and last to getting the therapist down, along with anyone else in their worlds who counts. Fritz submits that they are detectable fairly easily and early. They indicate their presence usually during the initial session by their smirk, or by the mouth which appears to smile while the rest of the face does not. The smirk often remains while various forms of hostile behavior appear, making for a red-flag phenomenon. The patient is busy pretending what he does not feel and sending concurrent incongruous messages. The hostile ones win out. And Fritz returns now in memory saying again, "Watch for the person who imagines something, then pretends to feel it." In contrast, people of relative good will, whom Fritz calls "nurturing," use their social roles and game playing (in addition to manipulation) as vehicles for bringing forth their feelings. Their roles provide a structure or a known way of experiencing and expressing themselves, rather than a pose for the purpose of seducing and defeating.

The bear trapper cons us with offers of gifts and nurturing. His payoff is withdrawal. He operates in a repetitious pattern: he invites us in, waits until we get almost there, then he slams the door. He offers himself; his love, joy, sex, whatever we want, stays around while we respond a bit. Then suddenly he withdraws and is gone, leaving us bewildered and isolated. Consider, for example, premature ejaculation or the vanishing business partner who leaves as the payoff approaches, the person who repeatedly leaves emotionally after inviting involvement, the chronic breaker of dates, the patient who shows great promise and abruptly destroys what he has gained. The bear trapper seduces often with beguiling charm before producing his quick, unannounced shift in behavior. In instances of major, permanent withdrawals, the person who is the object of the performance is apt to feel stunned, perhaps with the thought that he himself must be crazy. Friedrich Hear writes of the twelfth century teachings of the Empress Matilda to her son Henry: "(She) had brought up her son on a precept taken from the art of falconry. 'Show your friends and allies their reward, keep it dangling before their eyes, but remove the bait before they can seize it . . .' There were obvious risks in following such advice, which imposed an intolerable strain on both parties to the sport; Henry died an exhausted and embittered man."[4] Learn to recognize the falcon early. The price of his offering is emotional bankruptcy.

I am hearing Fritz, repeatedly and unequivocally, "Do not begin work with the poisonous person. There is only one course to follow. Leave him." My experience is a bit less absolute. I have seen people present initially a fair amount of poisonous behavior and have continued to work with them, ultimately with enough success to justify the effort. At the beginning with these people, I am seeing some promise in them beyond their attempt to frustrate me. If I get in touch with my own wanting to go to work despite the presence of a significant component of "poisonous" behavior, I show the patient from the beginning that I will not be sucked in. I tell him that I am not entirely hopeful that he really wants to or will do anything of worth for himself. I convey unmistakably with words and my total behavior confirms that I will not continue to work with him if his energy goes primarily into frustrating me. We succeed if he then elects to give up some of his defeating behavior and finds more willingness to work honestly.

As we consider these familiar patterns from the human scene and reflect upon some of their implications, I want to state the obvious. Each one of us has in his potential behavioral repertoire all of these ways of being. We differ in the percentages of what we elect to express. In the event of significant toxic behavior, the therapist confronts two issues: he must answer for himself and in his own interest, how much negativity he will tolerate and cope with, and he must assess the patient's components of manipulation to defeat and good will from the point of view of possible intervention through therapy.

## CHAPTER TWO

# The Work of the Therapist

## Perceptions of the Therapist

Let's imagine meeting the patient for the first time. Begin by observing, and note especially:

*The relational-withdrawn dimension.* Look for contact. How much is he willing to experience? How much of himself? How much of his world?

*Holes in the personality.* Look for avoidance and statements of helplessness. How much and which parts of himself have been lost?

*The voice.* Identify his major social roles. How much authenticity does he show?

*The good will-poisonous dimension.* Key to workability. Does he reveal some willingness to cooperate?

We find, hopefully, that the patient is willing to be at least somewhat in touch with his own process and with his environment, that his avoidances are less than continuous, that his voice is not totally phony and that he reveals some honest feeling. We now have something with which to work. We wait, seeing and hearing, for the emergence of the specific phenomenon which indicates to us something of what the patient is about. As we remain available for whatever unresolved material the patient may allow to become foreground, we are with him, in the present, being whatever we are, allowing ourselves to be aware of what is obvious in his behavior. We proceed from the basic assumption of Gestalt theory that through his awareness of sensation the patient's urgent unfinished experience becomes evident and available to him.

Perception has an object. That object or phenomenon has an existence which can be validated, and it is with this, the observable data, that the Gestalt therapist involves himself. His eyes and ears are instruments of perception for discovering what the patient reveals and for registering what is compelling. The event which we perceive to be foreground becomes, *as it exists*, the focus of our attention. We are interested not in subjecting this aspect of the client to the scrutiny of our intellect, but rather in the simple acceptance of its existence. We touch the primary behavioral events not with our minds but rather through our awareness. We want not to close out these events with an explanation; we prefer to open them up for the process of discovery.

The observable happening, the existing phenomenon, simply is: it stands alone. Beyond what we experience through perception, there is nothing more. We can add something from our thinking if we like, as long as we do not confuse our own offering with the process of the experience, and as long as we judge this intellectual contribution to be of sufficient worth to justify interrupting the flow of experience. I believe that for most of us it takes a long time to know experientially what the phenomenologists have to give us. "A rose is a rose is a rose," Fritz is quoting through our days at Lake Cowichan. And while we are here, I am returning to one special evening at sunset as Fritz walks toward my cabin and I go out to join him for a walk. We are alone and quiet, moving slowly now up hill a bit, our arms linked. Now I leave the twilight and Fritz and our movement and get into verbalizing a program for the future. He continues on, his arm still firm and his pace undisturbed, and I know that he is present. He remains quiet. He prefers not to interrupt his experience.

## Discovery

We set out to allow the patient to discover. To discover again, as he is willing, some parts of himself and his power which are now alien and not available to him. Now the Gestalt basic assumption is: "Learning is discovery." Whatever the therapist does to interfere with, impinge upon, or diminish the process of the patient's discovering-for-himself assures that to that extent no therapy occurs. Discovery is the heart of the growth process and the essence of psychotherapy. The role of the therapist is to facilitate and not to teach; to "be with," not to impose. He uses his imagination to devise situations in which the patient can explore and find for himself new dimensions of experience.

This is to say that the therapist is part of the background of the patient's working. He acts as the catalyst who provides a series of situations. He is continuously involved in the challenge of providing a "new" place, moving with the flow and change of the patient to create the background which facilitates this person's continuous becoming. If the therapist fails in this task of providing a place where the patient finds his environment different from what he has known and evoking of new responses, discovery does not occur and the patient leaves as he entered.

In his role as background or as catalyst as the patient works, the therapist is engaged in producing ideas, in making suggestions, and in creating existential situations for the patient to fulfill. These ideas derive from the therapist's perceptions of the patient, his awareness of his own responses, his memory and imagination, along with his knowledge of how therapy works. Tapping all these resources, the therapist devises designs to facilitate and encourage the patient's exploration of areas and experiences which have long been forbidden.

Fritz distinguishes two basic ways of working: becoming the facilitator and taking an active role himself in the patient's work. In the latter event, the therapist is not part of the background but rather is one of two principal actors. His role then becomes equally as much foreground as that of the patient. Fritz points out that the therapist must understand and decide whether or not the therapeutic task can be accomplished by facilitating alone, or whether or not it is necessary in addition to take an active role with the patient.

Among my poignant and unforgettable memories of working with Fritz, I find him playing the obsequious servant, the complement to my "snob" and "lady" roles. Apparently, such high drama was indicated for getting beyond my lifelong blinders in relation to these roles. Surely, as he works with me, Fritz must indeed see and hear, get in much with his own feelings and involve his imagination, knowing that in this instance facilitating is not enough. If I am to grow beyond this determined and unaware production of "lady," he must take an active role. He does. Everybody at Lake Cowichan appears to be awed by Fritz's very active portrayal of .the obsequious servant! Beyond feeling awed, I am dumbfounded, anxious, lost, angry, convinced for a while that one of us is crazy. After I let go of all this and I've learned how one feels approaching a major impasse, Fritz tells me that I've still a way to go and that I can continue my journey by running the grocery store in his proposed new community. I am touched, and for a long time I think often of the grocery store.

Fritz's ideas and elaborations of the principle of discovery are in many ways unique, I believe, and sometimes at variance with practices evolving from the traditional psychoanalytically-oriented method of working. Allowing the patient to discover for himself is not compatible with the therapist's making interpretations or with his inexplicitly relying on his own fantasies. Our presenting our interpretations to the patient obstructs discovery in several ways, any one of which precludes the very process we hope to achieve. With his interpretations the therapist reassures the patient of what he already believes, that he is underdog to the therapist who knows more and is more powerful. With the intellectual mode of explanation, he encourages the patient to stay in his head, promoting DMZ functioning rather than feeling experience. He confirms that he is active and the doer; the patient a passive recipient. And when he interprets the therapist robs the patient of his chance to discover by "getting there first." The therapist claims the discovery, which then becomes his gift to the patient.

"Interpretation" actually has to do not with the client but with the therapist. He brings forth his own fantasy, labels it fact, and hands it (perhaps with pride) to the client. To avoid such imposing of himself upon another human being, the therapist has simply to be aware of himself. He knows when he is in touch with his feelings and when he fantasizes. His fantasy is his own production, and may or may not be of some intellectual interest to the client. The therapist's fantasy provides one indispensable tool for working, of great worth as long as this creation is not confused with the self of the patient. The Gestalt therapist produces fantasy deliberately for the purpose of devising a scene for the client. We provide a stage and the props, sometimes a character and a chorus, where someone else can play out his own preferred roles and where he can exchange with that part of his existence which he projects onto the world. Through the therapist's fantasy emerges a world where the "victim" can find and then become his persecutors, the "preacher" his congregation, the avoider his pursuers. The client works and discovers through his experiencing within the scenes of his existence.

We enlist our fantasy for whatever effort of facilitation. At Lake Cowichan one sunny morning Fritz presents a setting. From the background of my imminent leaving after a month in this wonderland of Vancouver Island, to go home to the Bay Area for a few days, I'm stuck. No longer fully here nor yet wanting to leave for there. Here with a few people in Barry's cozy cabin by the lake, I'm feeling out of touch and ineffectual. Fritz gives me a store. I see it immediately, clearly. A big store with all kinds of offerings. Fritz asks what is for sale in this store, and tells me to choose something. I go to the bicycles, hesitate a moment between two and then give up my immobilizing as I get in touch with my preference. In Fritz's fantasy place, with him, I'm willing to move again. I'll take the blue bicycle. And after this, I'll take also the airplane to San Francisco.

I am remembering again Fritz's words, and his emphasis, "You *never* know more than the person in the hot seat." My imaginings are not a source of information about the patient's inner experience. I believe that implicit in Fritz's teachings is an injunction to the therapist. It has to do with humility regarding one's own fantasies, with knowing the limitations of their usefulness and understanding their inherent potential destructiveness. Playing the role of therapist involves a commitment to use my fantasy knowingly and with discretion.*

## Taking Responsibility

In the process of his discovering himself, and as an inseparable adjunct to it, we ask the patient continuously to take responsibility for himself. We have set the stage already. The therapist's behavioral statement, "I will be with you. You will do what you find necessary," along with his eschewing the role of helper, leaves the patient in charge of himself. The therapist establishes a consistency wherein he accepts responsibility for all of his own behavior and rejects any responsibility for the patient, a way of being with someone which transmits expectation through experience —experience which the patient then checks out and attempts to reverse. The critical variable in all of this is that the therapist recognizes how the patient cons and manipulates and demands in his determination that the therapist will play the powerful one and solve the whole thing. The therapist has at this point three immediate tasks; to recognize how the patient tries to get support from others rather than to provide his own, to avoid getting sucked in and taking care of the patient, and to know what to do with the patient's manipulative behavior.

The implicit statement of the patient at this point is roughly: "I can't cope, in this and this situation, and you

---

* Sartre writes of our knowing the other "(who is) a connected system of experiences out of reach . . . But to the extent that I strive to determine the concrete nature of this system of representations . . . I radically transcend the field of my experience. I am concerned with a series of phenomena which on principle can never be accessible to my intuition, and consequently I exceed the lawful limits of my knowledge."[5]

can. I 'need' you to show me the way, so that I can go on with my life." This is sometimes not much life at all, but rather an existence which includes a succession of propositions submitted by the patient to people who like to take over the management of others. The therapist is merely the latest try. Hopefully, "the buck stops here."

We see here another radical departure from the format and procedure of traditional therapy, which speaks often of "the needs of the patient." The therapist implies and appears to believe that the patient "needs," in the sense of "must have in order to survive." I hear this phrase spoken, "the needs of the patient," referring to demands which the patient makes of people in his world, including the therapist, for emotional support. Fritz makes a major contribution with his unequivocal distinction between needing and wanting. In order to make evident and explicit to the patient his implicit demand, cloaked as "I can't cope and so I need . . .," ask him, "How do you need?" If he is willing to hear himself and to explore further this business of "needing," he can discover that he means that he "wants." And he can come to understand that he uses "need," with its connotation of survival, to try to control the therapist. The patient must discover as a basic condition of his taking responsibility for himself when his "needing" amounts to avoidance with built-in manipulation. Our bodies "need" (water, food, rest, oxygen, temperature) for survival, and our emotional beings "want" from others, and can if necessary exist in the face of another's refusal to give.

Continuing with fundamental issues involved in the patient's learning to be increasingly responsible for himself, we work with his verbal means of avoidance and specifically with impersonal pronouns and verbs employed in the passive voice. We hear the patient first depersonalize himself into "it" and then become the passive recipient of the vicissitudes of a capricious world. "I did this" becomes "It happened." I find that I must interrupt people repeatedly, asking that they own themselves. We cannot work with what occurs somewhere else and happens to one. And so I ask that they find their way from, "It's a busy day" to "I keep myself busy," from, "It gets to be a long conversation" to "I talk a lot." And so on. The other overworked verbal cop-out occurs with the substitution of "can't" for "won't." The patient expresses and he experiences that he can't. *Can't* tell you how I feel. *Can't* get up in the morning. *Can't* remember. As long as the therapist accepts the patient's statement of disability, both are stuck. The first steps of the way out occur when the patient begins to discover and then to accept that behind his helplessness lies unwillingness. Ask him to hear himself through becoming the other person, feed back, mimic, share feelings, play the opposite role, whatever it takes, until the patient discovers his avoidance and is willing both with his words and beyond the verbal level to take responsibility for each fragment of his behavior, however abortive, "unintentional" or unacceptable he finds it.

## The Sequence of Avoidance, Anxiety, Awareness

Both discovery and taking responsibility for ourselves depend upon being in touch with what goes on outside of our intellects. Awareness is our means of discovery, of ourselves, and our worlds. Contact with the immediate flow of oneself and with events occuring around us provides the only possible basis for owning, accepting, being responsible for what we are, and for what we do. Looking at the other side of the coin, awareness is the object of avoidance. And more explicitly, the ultimate awareness which we seek to elude is inner experience. This is a decisive point with pragmatic implications. The patient believes usually that he avoids events (including human ones) in his environment. Once he discovers that it is his (imagined) feelings in response to these events that he runs away from, he is in a position to risk new experience. The external event perhaps we cannot change; his feelings, if he is willing, can be different. He now has a chance to give up running, to know and accept that which exists, and to discover that his feelings are, at the very least, bearable.

To work toward enhancing experience, we must first ask how awareness is being diminished. Since avoidance is a matter of minimizing awareness in order to preclude contact, and since anxiety is an indicator of avoidance, we are very much concerned in therapy with observing and working with the patient's anxiety and avoidance.

Sullivan first pointed out in his early work on special functions of anxiety that always anxiety is interpersonal. Add that anxiety relates to inner experience which is not yet occurring, but rather which the person anticipates and dreads. Fantasy, therefore, is a correlate of anxiety. The client must learn and understand this at the experiential level if he is to work effectively with his helpless roles. Anxiety then involves us invariably with the client's imaginings of doom. We are concerned with the content of his fantasy as he produces feelings of anxiety and with the "catastrophic expectation" whose function Fritz elaborates. In this context, the client must come to know the distinction between fear (which probably he often claims to feel and rarely does) and anxiety. Although the inner experiences may seem identical, the objects of fear and anxiety are different; one existing and the other imaginary. Fear occurs when there is an observable external threat present in one's world (a car racing toward him, a fire out of control); anxiety occurs when we produce fear-like feelings inside ourselves, and no external danger exists. If we ask the client to label his anxious feelings, we ask him implicitly to take responsibility for his fantasy and for responding to something which does not exist.

The point is, it seems to me, that we work with anxiety on two levels. We want to make explicit and to explore the component of imagination, the intermediate-zone functioning which poses the intolerable threat and which is the constant companion of neurotic anxiety. And we want to work through bodily awareness with the symptoms, those heightened uncomfortable physical sensations which the patient seeks to avoid. As he is willing to tolerate some discomfort and to take responsibility for producing these feelings, he can begin to discover how he goes about making himself uncomfortable. He allows his body to be as it is, learning through simple awareness of how he distorts his inner self, and the way is open for change to occur. In instances of significant anxiety which has existed fairly consistently over time, extensive work is required with fantasy and body awareness, all of which is integrated with the patient's existential problems. Even then the work is long and exacting and requires tackling in a series of different ways.

Fritz refers to anxiety as our elan vital or excitement. I like to think of anxiety as energy or excitement experienced at the unpleasant end of a continuum which extends in the other direction as well. Usually the patient indulges in avoiding the unpleasant feelings of anxiety, and in doing so detaches himself as well from a good deal of his energy. We want to provide a place where the patient becomes more and more willing to experience the unpleasant, in this case, his anxiety. When he avoids, we bring him back, and we stay with him. Once he begins to tolerate and stay in touch with his anxiety, he no longer opposes but flows with himself, so that he begins to move again. In giving up being stuck, he learns that he is not helpless. He knows now that he can survive the pain of anxiety, and he discovers the flow of himself. He experiences the power which comes with allowing that flow, this inherent characteristic of himself which is movement. The apparent paradox becomes clear, and is no longer paradoxical: "If I let be, I flow and change. If I attempt to control or to change myself, another part of me resists and I immobilize." And, returning to the original point of the patient's avoiding his anxiety, he receives a bonus. He has discovered how he can, by allowing some of the pain of anxiety, move on to other feelings. He cannot avoid going through what exists, but there is good news. He can get through it.

So we watch for the symptoms of the patient's attempt to evade some aspect of his situation. The various forms of observable behavior which emerge at this point are all variations on a single theme: departure from the here and now. We hear the patient change his voice and become phony, go into his head and produce streams of words. We observe that he shows signs of agitation, puts on blinders so that he fails to see the obvious, becomes silent and still and withdrawn, gets irrelevant, tries to suck us in with questions or with a brand new symptom. We want to experiment a bit first to find out whether he will get in touch with the phenomenon of his running away. We can facilitate his hearing and seeing himself and his expressing his inner experience; we can share our own response to his behavior. Will he hear and see if his behavior is reflected back? Will he act or play out his avoidance, given a situation, or get into a dialogue given an opposite? Will he allow the feeling he now experiences to take him back through time to another place and time, to learn of what was going on then? Hopefully, the patient discovers now three things: the fact of his going away, his method of avoidance, and the nature of that inner experience which he attempts to block out by avoiding some part of his world.

## Emptiness

There is another sort of blocking out of part of ourselves, which we experience as emptiness. In working with this special kind of emptiness, we are concerned with one of Fritz's concepts which I find immensely workable, "the sterile void which becomes the fertile void." The person literally experiences a hole, or space of nothingness within his physical being. He feels troubled and lacking—less than whole. We want to work toward the patient's using his own resources to achieve a transformation of this emptiness into substance.

We begin as always, where we are. Ask the patient first where it is that he finds that he is empty, and when he indicates (most often his chest and stomach areas), tell him to enter this emptiness. I've found, initially feeling somewhat surprised and pleased, that people usually cooperate quite willingly. The patient enters his emptiness. The difficulty arises a bit later, when he refuses to stay with the unpleasant phenomenon of his nothingness. Ask him to describe his experience, to express what he hears and sees (usually, but not invariably, blackness and quiet at the beginning), where he moves, how he feels, anything at all of his experience that he can share. We come now to a familiar place: the patient struggles and tries every way to avoid

**49**

being with what exists: we do what we can to block his avoidance and to be with him quietly when he is willing to let be. In this case to let his emptiness be.

If the patient is willing ultimately to give up his attempts to control and to accept his journey through his emptiness as it occurs, he will feel himself move without effort and in time he begins to discover. The blackness gives way to light and the void to a living world. More and more the patient sees a whole series or sometimes a kaleidoscope of his own creations, all unique and often beautiful. As he sees, hears, touches—still journeying through his void which he now makes fertile—he begins to respond emotionally to what he perceives. He has transformed his experience of himself from empty and depressed to vital, flowing, rich, and joyous.

I am remembering Fritz one evening at Lake Cowichan working with a man who begins by sounding halting, looking closed and producing very little to work with. He does expose his feeling of emptiness. Fritz asks that the patient enter his emptiness, and Fritz is clearly with him. Now the voice and the face of this man are changing suddenly, utterly. He shares with excitement and joy scene after scene of brilliant flowers and forests, all lush and vivid, and his creations are crowding fast upon one another. I find that patients who will endure the initial unpleasantness of the void to complete their journeys gain dramatically. They find a short cut. They experience themselves transformed from dejected helplessness into vitality and creative power which is so undeniable, that much gets accomplished in this single summary journey. And they tend to go on in the time that follows to risk significantly more.

## Skillful Frustration

Returning for a moment to the province of psychotherapy, which Fritz sees as the discovery and assuming again of lost parts of the personality or self, I want to state again the two basic tasks involved in fulfilling this mandate of psychotherapy. We want to fill up the holes or lost functioning in the personality and to identify and work with destructive social roles until the patient is aware of his manipulating, gives it up to some extent and allows himself to direct and rely primarily upon himself. We have just considered one especially direct and effective way of working, available to us when the patient experiences a void inside and allows this emptiness to become foreground. I want now to think about another route, this time in reference to role playing which obstructs the patient's access to himself. Fritz makes an invaluable contribution with his conception of the therapist's frustrating the patient. He presents a compelling case for the necessity of timely "skillful frustration" of the patient's manipulative roles.

As I've learned through watching Fritz (and through being his subject!) and in my working experience with other people, "skillful frustration" is a strategy ranging from the most abortive of gestures through a brief verbal message or angry confrontation to turning away into withdrawal from the patient.

The imperative has to do with timing. While we stop the patient here and there along the way as he wastes his time or avoids, we block him totally from taking refuge in old roles only as he approaches his impasse, a point by which he knows and understands very well indeed what he does. The therapist sees and hears the patient playing out his preferred and well-developed role in relation to worlds both real and imaginary, (that is, he acts out his existence). He hopes to be aware of what he feels and to remain impervious to the patient's attempt to con him into the game, and he hopes to find a way to block the merry-go-round.

I am returning to Fritz. Fritz is looking away quietly, his face inscrutable. Fritz is mimicking, ridiculing, and distorting the patient's behavior. Fritz is playing the opposite role; the role the patient tries to elicit from others, exaggerated to the absurd. Fritz is ever present on the patient's back, always instantly present to be in the way of the patient's next move. Fritz is showing, with his voice and his face, contempt and disgust. Fritz's voice is soft, with gentle mockery; his voice emotionless and his eyes direct as he states to the patient, "Now you are poisonous." Fritz is falling asleep. Fritz is angry, his voice hard. "You are totally phony." Fritz is just watching, waiting, refusing to respond. Fritz, the master skillful frustrator. For the rest of us, maybe not so masterful. it's a pragmatic affair. What works will do. We devise the behavior which hopefully both stops the patient now and contributes to a consistent, sustained experience of no way out. He must then act, out of his own creativity, on his own behalf.      /

I think of my friend and pilgrim-worker in therapy over some time, Jenny, and of how we came to the point where I knew that I must block her roles of helplessness. I turned my chair away and read a book and told her I felt tired of it all and in many ways I wouldn't listen. Jenny had avoided herself in therapy primarily through confluence. She became me. When she was blocked in the old way of pretending helplessness and she approached letting go, she dreamed of being on a path leading to my house, of walking a little and then stepping off the path to take another road and saying, "That is not my way." She told me that she knew now who she was not, and that she had found within herself, "...my friend, who knows what I need and want."

It seems to me very doubtful indeed that most patients will let go their victimizing roles without discovering on a deeply experiential level that with this behavior they go nowhere. I question how many of us who are stuck at the manipulative level will make the leap from the old way into finding our own way without the experience of finding ourselves blocked from the familiar route and so forced to turn to our own resources. In therapy, there is only the therapist to provide this experiencing of "nowhere to go." This comes from being blocked repeatedly as one does all the known things. There is only the therapist then to be silent so that the patient must in that last resort of aloneness discover that he is not after all abandoned. He has himself. He can, if he will, find a new way which comes from within himself.

## Verbiage, Lecture, Questions

Working as we do in the western world of the 20th century, we face all but continuously one particular form of avoidance: the ubiquitous functioning of the DMZ. If anything at all is to happen in therapy, we must find ways to frustrate the patient's stream of thoughts-flowing-into-words, the phenomenon of general verbiage which threatens to obscure all else. Fritz's injunction: "Do not be seduced by content," leaves open the way to respond to the patient's real message. Instead of getting lost in the labyrinth of his thoughts, we use our senses to be in touch with the obvious; with the sound of his voice, the movement of his face, his gestures or posture, his shiftings, his deadness, whatever behavior he produces most clearly. I think of a woman who remembers aloud an ordeal of long ago with her father. Shifting into dialogue, she speaks to her father, tearful, and explaining. And seemingly unaware, she moves her shoulders and shakes her head from side to side continuously. I respond to the movement of her head, and she exults instantly to her father, "I can say no!" In the moment of contact with her shaking of her head she discovers her message of "no" withheld, and her power to say it. She feels strong and rejoicing. Out of the memories of my own working long ago, I believe that response to her memories and her words would have left her anxious and stuck.

Let's go now to the major devices of verbiage for luring ourselves and others away from what exists in the now; specifically aboutism, the lecture, and questions. The assumption is that these verbal forms provide for roles of the avoider, top dog, and under dog.

Aboutism refers to the phenomenon of "talking about" the event, as opposed to experiencing, to DMZ functioning rather than being in touch. Fritz distinguishes the "explanatoriness" (the word even sounds like the deed) of talking about, from "understanding." Understanding comes only from experiencing the event, bringing to us that irrefutable knowing of having been there. We know the rose from seeing, smelling, touching. Anything more is "about" the rose and adds to our store of informational bits, but not to our understanding of the rose. I believe that only over a substantial period of time expanding awareness do more of us first differentiate aboutism from experience, and then begin to allow the balance to change in our daily living, giving up a bit of verbiage occasionally, for just being in touch and expressing. Talking about is a means of going after control. We can "broadcast" to avoid our feelings and so attempt to control our own beings. We can pour out streams of words and stay irrelevant, seeking to control the other person with our barrage of thoughts. Talking about can be aimed at hypnotising. We hypnotise with words, often in an attempt to establish that we are right. The role of the "district attorney" emerges as we list the evidence and establish our case against the other and for ourselves.

*Lecture.*   That special form of verbiage which is the lecture amounts to playing topdog. "Let me tell you how I—you should be, and how the situation is." If we decide against listening to the content of the lecture, we see the phenomenon: the person avoids dealing with his feelings by knowing everything, by adopting numbers of rules to draw upon, by playing the teacher. He avoids being with others by closing off his eyes and ears and staying closed up in his middle zone. Beyond his words, we are left with the phenomenon of being closed out by information. The lecturer responds to his pride, not to himself.

And I return to Fritz's words citing a life devoted "to actualize a concept of what one should be like, rather than to actualize oneself."[6] Recognize the topdog player who attempts to control with his rules as the patient who must, if he is to grow, find a place in therapy where he will begin to allow the situation to control. For giving up control, Fritz gives us the village idiot. He reminds us that the village idiot no longer has any "shoulds." When we lived together at Lake Cowichan, he asked us to play the village idiot regularly, all of us at once. We did and movement and sound prevailed, and this was a way toward feeling released and quiet and letting be, for all of us verbalizing topdog players together.

*Questions.*   Fritz submits that questions constitute a unique variety of verbiage reserved for a special suck-in. He points out that questions have a hook on the end. The seduction of the questioner seems to be aimed at the listener's pride, underdog addressing topdog. Fritz is saying, "Only children ask questions." And I hear someone question Fritz, and I see that he simply gives no reply at all nor any indication that he even hears the question. Hearing the patient's questioning, we have also an alternative which is to ask him to make a statement of his question. Whatever is behind the question is then revealed, and the patient has an opportunity to deal with it himself. The underdog-to-topdog game is averted, and the patient experiences his ability to get for himself what he wants.

Two other aspects of verbiage as questions are the why-because rationalization game, and the game of the helpless killer. In the first instance, the question invites intellectualization. The questioner demands an "explanation"; the answerer goes into his head, invents a hypothesis, and submits it as justification, excuse, rationalization. "Why-because" retreats to the DMZ to avoid what exists. In another arena entirely, the defeater is into a different game with his questions. He lures the other person through his questioning appeal into responding with ideas or information, then uses the answer to ridicule, put down, prove the person incompetent. We recognize in this maneuvering a favorite devise of poisonous behavior.

## Stuck Points and the Impasse

Returning to the time in the course of therapy when we must find ways to frustrate the client. If we are successful in our attempts to block him, in preventing his taking refuge in accustomed roles, he will experience having nowhere to go, or being stuck. We have been working toward this point of impasse, the place where the client experiences that he cannot move on. Fritz means to convey through the word "impasse" the experience of the client when he no longer finds support from a source outside of himself and he has not yet discovered how to rely upon himself. At this time, since he has no remembered experience to the contrary, the client believes that he is actually without the necessary inner resources to provide for himself what he requires. In order to maintain his status of impotence and dependence, he is committed absolutely to believing that no new ways exist, and certainly that no new power of his own providing is available to him.

The client works enormously hard at keeping his dilemma unresolved, especially by making himself inaccessible through exhaustion, confusion, being lost, and producing all sorts of anxiety. So, especially now, the therapist must provide a special place. First of all, we want to encourage the person to let be and to allow his being stuck, including all of the painful feelings involved. We want to discover more and more about how he immobilizes himself. If this deepening of his experience occurs, he is in touch with more of himself, he allows more suffering, he approaches more closely the point of giving up trying to control.

We want at this time especially to work explicitly with that constant variable of the impasse: fantasy. The phenomenon of being stuck involves responding to one's fantasy. The patient believes that he cannot do what is necessary for himself in this situation as a function of imagining that he cannot, and then establishing his imaginings as immutable fact. Further, he secures his already entrenched position with threats to himself of catastrophe, should he attempt another course. He articulates a rationale which projects the origins of his fantasies of doom onto the world: "I'll be fired from my job"; "My children will suffer"; "People will have nothing to do with me." Whatever the words and ideational content, the immobilizing threat distilled to its essence presents an issue of survival. The patient imagines that somehow he will no longer function or be all right unless he continues exactly as in the past. "At least this way I can get by." Should he risk the unknown, he cannot imagine a comfortable or appealing future or even see that he can continue to exist. He will die. Our task is to facilitate the patient's discovery that he operates on the basis of a creation of his imagination, invented for the purpose of insuring that he does not shift into asserting himself out of his own being. His craziness lies not in his fantasizing or make-believe roles or in his manipulations, but in his failure to distinquish his imaginings from what exists in the world. "The insanity is that we take the fantasy for real."[7]

Fritz seems to cite as the means of recovery this single condition: recognize the impasse as a construct of fantasy. The sequence does not follow invariably. Not everyone wants to get through the core of his neurotic problem. After we have traveled the course of the road map of therapy, fulfilling the preceeding levels of neurosis, we confront the major impasse. Getting through this impasse, or letting go of the manipulative level, does not in my experience necessarily follow recognition of the role of one's fantasy. I do not find that the patient's learning how he is stuck, that is, his gaining full awareness of his impasse as a fairy tale web mistaken for reality, leads necessarily to his giving up his constricted existence and going on to trust himself to direct his own life. The whole issue of getting through the impasse remains to me largely enigmatic. It seems after all the being with and struggle and work and resulting new awareness and ways of being, simply that some people will and some will not make the fundamental shift into self-reliance. Some patients part with their fantasy and put aside their controlling to trust themselves to assert what they are and to cope out of their own resources. They give up functioning out of anxiety and negativity to follow their own imperatives. Others, with full awareness that their loss amounts to much of their potential authentic life, prefer to continue to bypass their own inherent wisdom and to pay the price of enduring the constraints of their private, imaginary worlds.

Among reasonably healthy, bright people with neurotic problems, perhaps those least willing to risk what seems at the time to be everything, to go through their impasses, are those most caught up in struggling at a deep level to get what they want and fend off what they don't want. I am thinking of the quality of experience which Ronald Laing[8] has called "ontological insecurity," or the most minimal trust in oneself to get by and in others to be on one's side or even neutral. Securing validation and some small degree of nurturing, and guarding against imagined overwhelming, if not annihilating intrusion, then become the business of living. In many situations, regardless of outward appearances as to what else may be giong on, the patient's energy goes into an exchange with others which is pulling in and pushing away in order just to maintain the imagined necessary edge of safety. For these people whose existence is largely given over to observing security measures, much work is necessary in therapy over a substantial period of time. And I believe that for them the anxiety which occurs unavoidably at the point of impasse presents on the experiential level a special hazard, since what is now required of them is to endure the very threat which their daily effort has been committed to avoiding.

I think of people coming from such struggle who have worked in therapy with me long and well, and who "know" in their heads and some levels beyond that their threats are imaginary. These are people who have taken risks and changed their lives impressively, finding a new, largely positive way, and who now approach the major impasse.

I am thinking of Joan, who left therapy a year or so ago, before confronting her impasse, feeling assertive and enjoying her life. Now she returns saying, in the most poignant possible language, "The core of me didn't get cured."

I think of Joe, who increasingly gives up his lifelong role of the oddball who, sometimes imagining that he may disappear and feeling "frantic" inside, disconcerts by demanding attention which he then doesn't really want. Joe works with his problem of occasionally making his mind blank when someone looks at him, so that his mind will not "get taken over." He has risked experiencing many lesser impasses along the way, so that he has come to know intimacy and sustained feelings of success.

And Beth, whose victimizing, manipulative role speaks to me, referring to her "trusting" self: "I'm all she has ever known. I've been on my own since first grade. I know what's best for her, and I don't like people acting caring and warm. I let her have some good feelings sometimes, and she feels like a warm bath when people are kind. But then I tell her they don't mean it. They will only use her eventually. You don't know me as well as she does. I'm all she has." Beth has achieved much professionally, and her growth in authenticity and risk taking brings her ever increasing fulfillment. Like Joan and Joe, she is a courageous worker and brings all of her strength as she faces her impasse, as she faces giving up, "all I've ever known."

## Avenues for Moving On

There are some things we can do among the group of those willing that can perhaps increase the percentages of people who get through the impasse. These procedures are intended to facilitate the patient's acceptance of his situation and feelings at a given moment; his beginning to move again with his natural flow, and his taking ever more responsibility for himself as a precondition and correlate of discovering that he does indeed fashion his own existence.

First, there is the importance of being satisfied that the patient really *is* stuck before we introduce facilitating measures. Beware of rushing in to assist the progress. When the patient moves by himself, producing, using his awareness of himself or of his world, exploring, he is already doing exactly what we hope for. From time to time, and not so infrequently, I am amazed and admiring of how little some people require from me. Some patients work quickly, profoundly, getting through most parts of their therapy with minimal active participation from me. They seem to be with themselves and with me easily, flowing from the now into the next step of their work. With these people I intervene for the most part only when I see that they are wearing their blinders. I am hearing Fritz telling us to recognize what the patient is willing to do for himself. Fritz is repeating again and again: "Don't push the river; it flows by itself." I am remembering, too, Fritz's waiting—waiting for the other person to produce some behavior that can be used; to produce on his own. The basic assumption for the Gestalt therapist is that the therapist can do no more than to be available. Anything else is interfering.

We arrive at the time when the patient has done all that he knows to do, he is wanting to move on, and he feels stuck. (It seems to me worth stressing the component, "wanting to move." Without the split, including the energized as well as the immobilized side, we have no behavior to work with.) Let's put aside for the moment any detailed considerations specifically involving splits and polarities and projection. Let's look first at procedures available to the therapist as facilitator when the patient feels stuck and in conflict.

I like to begin by finding out just where the patient is. As he describes his impasse, expressing how he feels stuck here and now, ask him to take responsibility for immobilizing himself and for wanting to stay where he is; that is, for creating the feelings he expresses. Often at this point he responds also as his opposite or active self, exposing objections to being stuck, and a dialogue between the polarities is possible. Another possibility for getting some movement going is his shifting between the present situation and fantasy places. Ask him to express what he hears and sees, then to close his eyes and go away into himself or his fantasy. If his perceptions heighten and feelings emerge as he experiences alternately the two places of contact, introduce again some aspect of his stuck point. It seems to me now that it is something like not pressing one's luck. A few moments ago the patient faced his impasse and would do nothing. Now he moves a bit. I find that if I select from the total scene of his stuck point just one aspect, usually he will accept this fragment and continue to move, and so he begins to involve himself again with his existence. For example, if the patient is stuck in unwillingness to let go of some part of the past and feeling lonely and lost, as he begins to move, introduce not the critical aspect—the person who has gone away—but some related condition of his existence such as his empty home in the evening. Sometimes the patient will respond with feeling to seeing his old, familiar existence (the place where he is stuck) imagined on the empty chair before him. One alternative is a dialogue with his existence; another is to create alternatives to or modifications of his existence which he can then experience. Sometimes the patient who resolutely resists his own existential dilemma is willing to become involved in a fantasy situation drama which we can devise to parallel his own.

Although he is stuck, the patient is rarely entirely subdued to the extent of producing no observable behavior. What does his body say? Discover what he *is* doing, however abortive or controlled. Ask him to exaggerate his limited movement, of which he may well be unaware. In this way he begins to be in touch with and attend to some energized behavior. Deliberate exaggeration goes along with and strengthens what already occurs, enhancing the force of spontaneous flow against constriction. When the patient appears to be tensing a muscle, suggest that he move with what he does already by pulling in even more, until he can constrict no longer, then let go. Sometimes it is necessary for him to repeat this sequence of pull in-let go several times before he will permit involvement of other parts of his body and finally achieves autonomous bodily and emotional expression. As he works, direct his attention to his breathing. Explore how he uses his breathing to immobilize himself by allowing only shallow movements which severely restrict the amount of air he gets. If we do not breathe, we see to it that nothing much can occur.

Attend to whatever unfinished business the patient reveals. Does he stop himself by introducing repeatedly something with which he then refuses to stay? Is he aware that he keeps around a situation with which he will neither cope nor part, but which he drags in for distraction and hassle? When he seems to be stuck with unexpressed negative feelings toward someone, have him use Fritz's resentment sequence. Ask him to express to the other person first his resentments, then his demands. Next, have him take responsibility for his own expectations. This procedure provides a way to begin where the patient frequently is (stalled in his own resentment and silently playing the blaming game), and to progress through authentic open messages of what he wants, to his owning his expectations. He moves from attempting to get what he wants from others through resentment to expression of himself as he is and willingness to find a way himself toward his own fulfillment. And now he accepts implicitly that in relation to another, through asking clearly for what he wants, he does all that he can. He has "finished." The other person may give or may withhold, and the patient may stay or move on. With or without the other, he finds a way. Resentment recedes into the background, the Gestalt is completed, and the patient is open again for a new part of himself to emerge.

At this juncture what may emerge is a new obstacle. The patient finds another way to stop himself. The burden is now off the original object of resentment and onto someone or something else. Once again we are immobilized, and now the behavioral phenomenon becomes one of the patient's holding tightly to his status quo. First, we must work through the current blaming game, going to whoever or whatever the patient now brings in as the impediment. When he has reached the point of knowing and acknowledging that he arranges to stay where he is, we want to be again as deeply and fully as possible in the place of impasse. The patient probably has still some discovering to do in the area of what he gains from remaining here.

I want to summarize a recent working session with Susan which offers an instance of self-torture and staying stuck. She has clung for 10 years to a pseudo-relationship with Jim. Little happens. She is mostly emotionally dead, out of touch with her anger and sex. She finds just barely enough nourishment in being with her friend to survive emotionally. The arrangement takes her time and her energy and assures that she will not be in real touch with much of the rest of the world.

In therapy the patient discovers that relatively little of her self is involved in any kind of living. Through her holding onto this one relationship, she controls also the rest of her life. Her friend continues with his favorite topdog roles—demanding much and giving little. The patient protests such cruelty, with words and with tears, but continues to hang on and to suffer.

Finally one day the patient has temporarily abandoned her depression game, feels some strength and feels "like doing something:" She realizes that she feels no anger toward her friend even as the psychic blows continue.

We put the patient's missing anger on the empty chair and she begins a dialogue. As she takes the chair to become her anger, her voice changes, becoming a toneless low monotone. She slumps slightly. I ask her to let her body slump over as much as she wants to. Her head goes down; her shoulders forward, and she slides down in the chair, stating, "I feel myself becoming nothing." After a bit I ask the patient to shift to the other chair and use her eyes and ears. She says to "angry Susan:" "I hear you and see you making yourself dead." She sees her avoidance into deadness to maintain what she has with her friend, and her use of her friend to stay dead. She goes easily into the past and into ten years of deadness.

As she travels back through the accumulated years her voice becomes louder, more forceful, and begins to sound angry. Since Susan appears to have taken back some of her anger and is willing to express it, I want to use her new integration and increased power to explore what she is willing to do in her existence—with her friend. She puts Jim on the empty chair, and immediately she begins to withdraw into deadness again. "I will be alive and angry within myself, only dead and depressed with you."

At this time I set up a situation for Susan where she can easily experience herself in either of the two roles she has introduced: the somewhat angry Susan or as depressed and helpless. Nearby we have another chair for her friend, who can then be introduced when she wants to be with him, either as the deadened suffering victim or as her active self. For the rest of the session, Susan shifts between her in-touch and out-of-touch roles, learning by switching chairs how fast and often she goes back and forth, and experiencing how she uses her body to change roles, and effecting some integration. She gets involved with Jim in both roles, discovering that when she becomes dead with him, she is now sometimes willing to move through her depression into feeling of sadness and anger. She now makes an important discovery: her active, feeling self retreats when given power, and so operates in collusion with her helpless role to keep herself involved with Jim. The patient is not, at this point, feeling herself belonging in either chair. "I'm in the middle." I ask her to sit down in the middle between her two roles. She says to her friend from there, "I want to pull back from you and I am not yet ready to have you go away. I want to keep torturing myself for now." She takes responsibility for immobilizing and depressing herself and she knows a good deal about how she goes about maintaining her underdog role. She knows absolutely that at this time she will not be anywhere except where she is. It is only from this position of awareness that she has much chance of going on.

Let's turn back to specific resources which are available to help meet the challenge of the client who feels split and immobilized. Travel back through time. When the patient experiences some feeling and also seems not to be going anywhere, ask him to let his feeling take him back through time and see where he goes. Often he will readily find himself in a situation of long ago which is also the scene of his existence, and where his role and his feelings are identical with those currently obstructing his life. In the newly-discovered context of long ago, he may be more willing to experience himself and to work. Traveling back through time along the path carved out by emotion makes for a powerful and productive journey. I think of a young man whose existence had been a series of moves, of continuously changing apartments and jobs and people. One day he had the good luck (sense?) to wear his sandals instead of shoes to the office so that I could see that at times he wiggled and curled his toes. Being largely out of touch with his body, he knew nothing of the movement of his toes, let alone their message. When he became his toes, that message turned out to be "I want to run." and he felt pronounced anxiety. His anxious feelings took him through the years directly to the third grade playground where he stood alone at the edge, watching the other boys play baseball. He was curling his toes.

The patient gets stuck in relation to his existence or some aspect of it. He will not move with his feelings and so be a part of his own situation. Have him then see his existential situation outside of himself on the empty chair, expressing to it whatever he is aware of feeling.* Sometimes when situational options occur, I like to bring in several

---

* Later on we will consider in some detail the use of the empty chair in relation to work with polarities. I am concerned now with only one rather specialized possibility having to do with the patient's feeling stuck in one of his roles.

chairs, imagining each alternative on a separate chair. The patient can simply let his various alternatives be, get involved with one of them, or explore his conflict by being with or becoming his available situations in turn. Several empty chairs are useful, too, sometimes for the patient's various roles. If he is stuck in one role, his others are then clearly available. Sometimes the patient will feel moved to get involved with another part of himself when he will do nothing with anyone else. Having these other roles "conspicuously" present helps. I do not remember that Fritz used empty chairs as vehicles for working through stuck points in just this way. The possibility occurred to me one day, and it has seemed to me to offer one more avenue of assistance. Sometimes people who come into the office weekly have special chairs which they designate for their various roles. They seem to use these physical places as emotional correlates especially if they feel stuck in one familiar role. I know something about where they are inside as I see where they sit.

Use fantasy choices. When the patient gets immobilized through torturing himself with alternatives and is unwilling to get in touch with his preference, suggest a fantasy trip which will involve his knowing and expressing a preference. If he seems reluctant to let go of a finished event so that he can move on, offer him a fantasy scene with many possibilities from which he can make a selection. If he finds contact and gets into motion in another place, perhaps he will carry that movement back into his present situation.

When the patient gets lost in torturing himself and shows little contact with his world, suggest that he do to someone else whatever he now does to himself. First, after identifying what he is doing to himself, go with rather than against the phenomenon by reinforcing his self-involved behavior. Then, after he has continued a bit to beat on himself, aware of what he does, ask him to do this same thing to someone else either in reality or in fantasy using the empty chair. If he makes his head ache, give him a pillow to imagine as someone else's head (preferably the object of his unexpressed anger) and treat it as he does his own. Fritz used to have people pushing various parts of his body. "Do this to me," I hear him say. If the patient gives himself a hard time, playing his own devil, have him torment someone else, or a succession of people. He will soon begin to feel more comfortable, stronger, able to move——often even enjoying himself. Especially people who prefer victim and good guy roles can learn what they least suspected about themselves.

Work with reversals. Ask the patient to play the opposite of the inner experience which he feels and won't relinquish. If he feels on stage and self-conscious, ask him to put his energy into his eyes and play the audience. If he feels left out and lonely, have him reject others. Sometimes —perhaps even often—people are reluctant to pretend deliberately to be what they do not feel. Sometimes they will go ahead if they are encouraged: "just pretend." And nothing is lost if they remain unwilling and still stuck. The odds for success seem good enough to opt for exploring the reversal procedure at times.

Another possibility to be used, in my opinion, with discretion and restraint: give the patient a phrase or sentence that supplies what he seems to imply or comes close to expressing spontaneously. How does he feel as he makes the statement? Does he find it to be true or not true? Will he adapt it, or make it his own? I think of a patient who reports that his head aches and pounds while his body from his neck down is still, inert, and waiting. I ask him to have a dialogue between his head and his body, and as his head expresses "ache" and "pain," I supply the words "energy" and "movement." He hears the words and makes his own use of them, going on to explore putting all of his energy into his head in order to control his body. Sometimes I supply people with whole sentences. Still, the caution we considered earlier in relation to using our own fantasy and interpretation seems to me to be indicated before we ask the patient to appropriate a statement that did not come from him.

As the patient approaches his impasse and finds new, sometimes tumultuous feelings arising which seem to be beyond his control, he strengthens his old familiar victimized role and experiences renewed helplessness. And so, as we see someone come very close to letting go of his old manipulative way, suddenly his pull to defeat himself reappears mightily, the world appears to be full of tigers again, and the struggle is intensified. At this point the patient can help himself by increasing the frequency of his working sessions, and I would surely hope for more than one a week. Getting through the impasse isn't easy, and we can at least make the special place available at this point on the patient's terms.

## Splits and Polarities

We come now to the subject of working with splits and polarities, which Fritz has called centering. As long as the client experiences only the extremes of any continuum, he has no center, no experiencing of a self which gives and takes on its own terms with the world. A middle-aged woman, feeling weary with unwanted work and battling children, finds herself split between opposite poles: "I hassle myself to get going in a hundred directions, and then I drink and do nothing." Topdog and underdog are at war, and we have a stalemate. The struggle is repeated without resolution. Most of this woman's energies go into a struggle for control of parts of herself, very little into allowing her organismic intuitive self to direct her to what she wants.

The work of the therapist now becomes that of facilitating integration and reconciliation of opposing parts of the personality. Our procedure involves dialogue as a means of getting two of the client's ways of being into contact with one another. They are now isolated, each waging its lonely battle for control of the personality. Dialogue between the roles which represent polarities opens the way for the process of mediation. Striving for control gives way to communication, and some yielding through consent becomes at least a possibility. The pathway toward integration of apparently exclusive differences is hearing. Fritz points out: "To listen, to understand, to be open, is one and the same thing." By identifying the client's polarities and then providing for the dialogue which can bring forth these two hostile roles, we create a place where the client grows more willing to relinquish his struggle for control, at least for a moment now and then, and to put some energy into listening and hearing.

The split may be between the client and another in his world whom he selects to play a complementary role, or it may occur within himself. Either way, the therapeutic procedure is the same.

First, the therapist must find the polarity. In order to become aware of how the client splits himself, the therapist allows himself to be open to the impact of the client's behavior. For one thing, this means resisting being lured into verbiage and content so that his energy is available for his eyes and his ears to perceive the basic phenomenon which the patient reveals. The crippling extremes of behavior which we want to extract are observable in what the patient does here and now in the therapy situation. He plays out, usually at first without awareness, one side and then another. As I see someone involved in creating one of his roles, I rely on my memory of other and opposite roles in his repertoire, bringing in appropriate past performances to introduce him to his polarities.

I am going back to a woman in the group workshop who wants to talk about the injustices perpetrated on her by her family. She invokes all reasonable and some elaborate protective measures, and still they find a way to do her in. Here and now in this room, beyond her verbiage, she plays out her roles of defeater and the defeated. She attempts to get us down by proving that there is no solution, not here through therapy, not anywhere. This woman brings to us her role of the helpless victim, and also its polar opposite, the "now-I've-got-you" downer who defeats by demanding the impossible. And this latter role, which is the critical variable, has to be pulled from the tangled web of overlay, the verbiage and the pose of innocence and the ploy of the helpless one just telling her pathetic story.

The universal polar opposites which appear in the guise of unnumbered specific roles Fritz has called topdog and underdog: roughly "shouldism" and "can'tism": "you should." "I can't." Topdog roles are distinguishable by their directness. Topdog controls by overwhelming: he lectures, bullies, threatens, knows everything, imposes his own rules on others. He uses words. He turns up regularly as parent, preacher, teacher, the Red Cross nurse, and the executive.

Underdog, on the other hand, attempts to control indirectly through passivity. He sabotages, forgets, arrives late and can't help it, tries hard and fails, puts everything off, gets confused, and stays uncommitted. Underdog is not to be found; he will not stand up and be counted. And always he can't help it. He deals in helplessness and avoidance, and he appears in characterizations such as "poor me," the victim, the child, "stupid," the virgin, the invalid, the martyr. When topdog and underdog get together, we have the time-honored arrangement of the frustrated master and the sabotaging slave.

Topdog and underdog roles are devised to gain control. The object is manipulation of oneself and others. We put together elaborate make-believe productions in the interest of getting what we want and avoiding what we don't want. The result is the same either way, through the approach of shouldism or the retreat of can'tism. Nobody gets anything authentic. Communication is blocked, and only the struggle for control remains. On the surface, topdog roles appear to be more powerful; in actuality, underdog roles usually prevail. Underdog simply goes away into avoidance leaving topdog frustrated. The obvious, or foreground phenomenon in the topdog-underdog struggle is "control madness," in Fritz's phrase, which results inevitably in the would-be controller feeling himself utterly controlled.

Find the polarity. I return to yesterday. Joe dreams of his exhaustion, feeling himself too tired to move, and suddenly standing over him is his opposite—the laughing and dancing Groucho Marx of inexhaustible energy. Back at Lake Cowichan, the nice guy, the gentleman who fulfills his obligations, discovers with Fritz his polarity as he plays the frustrator. And now we see face to face the somber predictable gentleman and the laughing saboteur. And I am seeing Jim as he reports his dream. He shows little vitality and his voice sounds dead. Then he lets us know that inside of his deadness he feels like a fool, and Fritz seizes the polarity, the corpse and the fool.

Having found the polarity, set up a dialogue, asking the patient to imagine that he sees and hears on the empty chair whichever role he now projects. Since we begin where we are, have the patient play first the role which he experiences at the moment. During the dialogue the work of the therapist is primarily to facilitate contact, which translated pragmatically means work with hearing. If in his separate roles the patient is willing to hear, we see his feelings begin to change and his split diminishes. He feels "together."

Most often people begin angrily to express themselves as one of their roles in relation to its opposite. They take the other chair then to respond, and I am reminded of the husband and wife who long ago stopped listening to each other. The client becomes each of these two separated roles by "talking at" the other. On the surface he appears to go along with my request, "Express this to him," but the real phenomenon is avoidance. In each role he maintains his isolation from the other as he avoids responding to what has been expressed on the opposite chair by reiterating his own performance. My intervention then is one of facilitating the client's recognition of his unwillingness to hear. "Are you hearing what he says?" Once he understands experientially the possibility of playing one role and also hearing the other, the client begins to respond with real communication. He moves fast toward increasing integration, and usually I do little more from this point on in his dialogue than to reinforce his growing power. This is often a matter of asking him to repeat again and more forcefully his own newborn spontaneous assertions of himself.

It is hard, I believe, to emphasize enough the importance of working toward the integration of fragmented hostile opposites, both as experienced within the personality and interpersonally. Some people prefer to play either topdog or underdog roles almost exclusively, so that for them the opposite is experienced consistently as existing in other people. In both instances, that of projecting one of the topdog-underdog roles and that of playing out both roles oneself, Fritz's concept of the hole in the personality obtains. In this case of polarities we have the critical hole; no center. The person has no way of experiencing himself as vitally involved in the world going on around him.

Discover where the patient experiences his power. I think of Larry who feels powerful as topdog. He plays the intellectual, then shifts to acting the frustrating playboy. He never quite manages to finish the work required for his master's degree; he fails to pursue to much length any of his involvements. On the one hand, he must work and study continuously; on the other, he must have a year off for sailing, backpacking, and wood carving. He begins his dialogue with a hostile exchange. *The Intellectual:* (sounding strong; posture upright) "I want *all* the time. I'm going to take six units. There will be time for only earning a living and study." *The Playboy:* "I'm tired of you. I want a year off. You won't give me anything." *The Intellectual:* "You're right. I want it all." As topdog, he experiences some power and his voice becomes lively and strong. He offers some vitality and access to himself. The power he feels now as topdog he can take into another situation. This can be a situation devised to put him into a place where the terms of his existence render him helpless ordinarily. So we have a chance to impart to a difficult area a spark of life brought back from topdog.

The right-left split is a particularly important one. Dreams especially reveal conflict experienced between our right and left sides in dramatically apparent and accessible form. The left side represents perceiving and feeling; the right side action, force, coping. Fritz points out that in schizophrenic conditions, one of these two ways of relating to the world is missing. The patient turns increasingly to feeling and has given up doing and coping, or he rushes into action which is not supported by perception. Reconciliation of right and left leads to achieving relationship and balance between doing and sensing. Not long ago I had the pleasure of watching a teenage boy restore his balance. He works with his "should-can't" split, becoming as topdog a devil who reviles and ridicules what he does. Underdog appears, suffering, sunk down into immobility. Then David discovers with a shout of triumph that as topdog he moves a great deal and feels almost nothing, and that in the opposite role he experiences no movement and overwhelming feeling. "What's missing and what I need is some of both!" And so he finds his own prescription and goes on toward implementing his balance.

And I return to left-right struggles with the memory of

another man concerned with his sexual problems. Characteristically he approaches a woman agonizingly slowly. Through the awareness continuum he gets in touch with startling left-right divergance, "like I have a line down the middle." His left side flows with feeling; his right side refuses to move. As he becomes each side responding to the other, his dialogue at first reflects antagonism and suspicion between his moving and his constricting sides, and then exchanges of giving and hearing begin to occur. His right side yields, and he experiences his body as less divided. Messages flow easily from one side of his being to the other, and finally his integrated self creates a moving, delightful sexual fantasy. He has achieved integration in the moment. He allows a new bodily integration which he can take from here, if he wishes, to its actual object: a real woman.

We find our power renewed as we achieve some integration of opposites, whether we begin with a split experienced within ourselves or with one of our polarities projected onto the world. As two of our roles which represent extremes of divergent messages begin to hear each other, we experience our strength more wholly. The "child" takes back some of his power from his "parents," the tortured from his devil. With fuller integration between the two positions, we experience our self or center. We can act among other people directly and in our own behalf, and we find that our manipulative roles are not so necessary. We know what we can do, and what we do not have to do. The problem lies in our preference to maintain our splits by empowering one aspect of our being almost exclusively. Energy flows to the parts of us with which we identify. In the western world today, overwhelmingly we want to own and give power to our intellects. In any opposing role, we tend to feel relatively helpless. And often as we exist today, the dictates of our intellect do stand in opposition to the yearning of our feeling life. And so Fritz's plea that we come to know some of our own strength also in integration with our deeper levels of feeling awareness. "Lose your mind and come to your senses."

Reconciliation of opposites may include forgiveness and letting go. I am now with Anne, who has worked in therapy over many months and seems to be stuck. She travels back again and again to become herself at eight years old when her mother admonished her: "Take care of your little sister and your father. And never, never go live with Marie," and then went out to kill herself. Anne plays her abandoned child role and her mother's role. She works with her child role in relation to her adult self, experiencing grief, rage, compassion, and frustration. She "understands" her existence as the helpless abandoned child and the premature parent who exists only to care for others. She experiences the usefulness to her now in terms of avoidance, of continuing to exist "as if" the child still lived. As she begins to find her own way through reconciliation of her roles of child and parent, she finds new trust in her own being. Feeling centered within herself, she is strong enough to forgive her mother, to let go of the attachment which provides the basis of her make-believe existence, and to let be; let herself be; let her dead parents be.

One final consideration of a critical form of splitting arises in the fundamental issue of discrepancy between how the patient appears to be and how he reports himself to be. At the very heart of therapy we find the issue of lack of congruence between the patient's outer or public realm and his inner or private one. We are concerned not with problems of appearance and being, but rather with two distinctive concurrent sequences of events in relation to one another. It seems to me that the classic mismatch or apparent lack of consistency which we see in the therapy situation occurs in the case of the patient who reports feeling agitated while he presents a picture of utter deadness. He experiences all kinds of unwanted excitation, anxiety, pain; we see and hear the stillness he imposes upon his chaos. The "obvious" or the phenomenon observable to our perceptions is only half the picture. So the actual phenomenon and the one to which we must attend in this case appears not in the deadness of the client, but rather in his lack of congruence. Our work lies with the issue of a splitting which obscures one of the two realities, rather than with the phenomenon created by observable behavior.

Ronald Laing makes the point with special clarity and

force in the context of his work with schizoid behavior. Referring to the dichotomy of inner or private events and outer or public ones, he emphasizes that in the first instance, the subject may or may not be aware and the observer is not aware; in the second, the observer perceives and the subject may or may not. Laing's point, which I've heard Fritz make indirectly and which I find to be crucial, is that we can never contact directly another human being's inner experience.[10] The patient is the authority and our single source of information concerning his consciousness of himself. Laing refers to the true self and the false self; the false self defined as those aspects of our being which are made available for observation and which do not correspond to our inner experience, while the true self is guarded and hidden. He asserts that it is the *relationship* between the two which is decisive, and that psychotherapy, if it is to be successful, must concern itself with the relationship between the observable, public person and the inner and hidden one.[11] Fritz provides the methodology and the tools to implement Laing's imperative. A major task of the therapist lies in finding the special split between the client's consciousness of his body and his emotions, his inner world, and his experiencing of the characteristic role which he plays in his existence, Laing's "false self." Then, through dialogue the client can establish for himself that what appears inconsistent really is not; (that the two ways of being do indeed support each other) and that what contradicts can be reconciled.

## Projections

Among the most dazzling of Fritz's illuminations of the dark, for me, is the matter of working with projections. Let's go back for a moment to some of his statements on the subject, and to the basic assumption of Gestalt therapy. Most of us have holes, or missing parts of our beings. These lost aspects of ourselves we experience as inabilities, and we reveal by avoidance and by our experiencing them as somehow outside of ourselves, usually in other people. As we have relinquished parts of ourselves by projecting them out into the world, we have separated ourselved from our power. Following these theoretical statements, the basic assumption of the Gestalt therapist is that most of this lost potential is recoverable through work with projections.

The work of the therapist in this area involves several aspects. First of all, to identify the patient's projections we have two major indicators. Anxiety and avoidance speak of what is missing in his personality, and his fantasies of the therapist's powers, presented usually in the form of demands, reveal the functions he imagines as occuring only outside of himself and therefore beyond his providing for himself. In relation to expressions and assertions of himself which the patient avoids, I want to determine the level at which he has stopped himself. Is he unwilling to reveal what he feels, so that he has lost touch with his means of expression, or has he given up his very feeling experience? If he no longer allows even consciousness of aspects of his emotional life, the problem shifts radically to one of his being-within-himself, and our work will be more difficult.

Having learned how the patient experiences himself as incomplete or unable by noting what is going on when he begins to avoid and by hearing what he looks for in us and through his report of his inner self, we can begin the work of having him take back aspects of himself which he has given away. We do this by asking the patient to become his projection. We give him a situation or a dialogue devised to include the role or the person he perceives as possessing his own lost part or function. Ask him then to play this part. Usually he protests at first, avoiding or resorting to trying to prove that he can't. He is being asked to risk the unknown, and he is anxious. Encourage him to explore some possibilities. If he is willing to play the new role, he discovers that he can become what he has projected, experience again what has been alien to him, own again the natural ability which he has denied. The function which was missing now occurs within him. He can do it! Once he has taken back from the world his own ability to feel, perceive, or perform, he begins to experience the newborn power of his expanded self. Give him opportunities immediately to try out and to enhance his re-owned ability and sensation and power with the group or with a succession of people on the empty chair. Give him what chance he wants to experience and to nurture this youngest part of him. I find much fulfillment in these moments of watching someone discover what he can do, of sharing his rejoicing as he affirms himself.

Become that which now you ask someone else to give you. I am remembering Fritz working with Joe, who has given away his ability to approve. Joe's missing part becomes clear as he turns to Fritz to be told that he is all right. First Fritz reinforces Joe's asking someone else for approval. Then Fritz has Joe become-by-playing approval, asking him to go to each one in the group and express approval to him. And I think of Sally yesterday, hiding and unwilling to reveal that she is the daughter of a wealthy father. She can't be seen. She has given up her exhibitionism. I ask her to be seen and seen in the forbidden role by playing Mrs. Got Rocks. Then I have her ask each group member to look at her while she demonstrates the extraordinary musicianship which is her great gift. Continuing work for Sally will be a dialogue using her own preferred role of the avoider who conceals, rarely initiates and feels little, and the part of herself which she has given away, the exhibitionist who enjoys being seen by others.

I want to summarize a working session which I had recently with a young married couple especially involving projection. John begins, stating that he has been in touch with avoiding Nancy. He reports that he stayed with his avoidance and unpleasant feeling and then discovered that he was angry. In touch with his anger, he perceived Nancy as infantile, weak, clinging to him "like she was plugged in to me as a plug goes into a source of power." Then John adds thoughtfully, "Living off of me," and he is quiet. He is remembering himself as a child. "This description fits me," he tells us.

Have John see on the empty chair the helpless, clinging image. He sees 12-year-old John looking downcast, immobile, and pitiful. Ask him to begin a dialogue with the helpless 12-year-old. Playing the helpless role, John first begins to feel confused. He asks me for confirmation and approval of what he is doing. I do not respond to his question. He then begins to assume a downcast position, being perfectly still except for moving his hands slightly. I ask him to become his hands and he discovers as his hands that he is soothing himself. He begins then to insist to John in the other chair that he can't stand the way he is and does not want to play helpless. Asked to get in touch with what he feels at this point, he replies that he is feeling anxious and uncomfortable. He attempts once more to get reassurance from me, then looks helplessly at John in the other chair saying nothing; looks down again. He is now stuck in his helplessness and confusion. I ask him to take the other chair and to hear and see the John he has just been playing. He looks and begins to laugh saying to grown-up helpless John, *"You're* doing it!" I ask him whether he believes adult John's words, that he does not want to be weak and clinging. The patient says no, adding, "that's just one more of his ways." I ask John to turn to his wife and say to her, "I really do want to play weak and helpless sometimes." He makes the statement to his wife, and he accepts responsibility further by elaborating his helpless performances.

In the course of his work so far John has seen his wife as disapproving; he has asked for her approval as well as for mine. I ask John now to hear himself giving away to his wife and to me his disapproval and approval. He acknowledges his fantasizing our approving of him and disapproving of him. I ask him now to see his wife and disapprove of her, then to disapprove of me and to imagine other people with whom he is involved on the empty chair and to disapprove of them. I ask him then to repeat this procedure, this time approving of each of us in turn. Readily, he becomes these projected parts of himself.

Turning to Nancy, I ask whether she had anything to express. She immediately gets into her anger at John, but stays with her anger only momentarily before she backs off into intellectualizations. With a bit more work she remains emotionally withdrawn, wanting to "talk at" her husband. Seeing her avoiding and stuck, I ask her to state her resentments to John. Nancy says with some feeling, "I resent you and dislike you very much when you are like that. You're wandering around, looking down, and moping and being helpless too much of the time." I ask Nancy then to make her demands of John. She replies, "I want you to be your own source of motivation. I don't want you hanging on me and I want you to supply your part of the money." I ask Nancy then to take responsibility for her own expectations and for their fulfillment. She says to him, "I want to live with a man who mobilizes and motivates himself."

Nancy and John express feeling relieved and feeling better toward each other. She takes responsibility now for her "should" fantasies of her husband. He works with his projections of his helplessness and approval, becoming more fully himself.

### The Voice

During the months at Lake Cowichan Fritz shared his conviction in many ways that if we were to work successfully, we must learn to hear. "A psychotherapist can work without eyes but not without ears." "Put your energy into your ears if you want to know what is going on." "I have one advantage over you; I hear more." "Words only lie and persuade; the message is the medium." "The voice is everything." Through these words I hear his voice, slow and steady, rising, falling, flowing.

Fritz is telling us two things: the voice is the carrier of the neurotic message and that unless we work with the sound of the voice as the perpetrator of defeat, the task of psychotherapy will not be accomplished. Regarding the first assertion, he reminded us that Jung's word for role playing or assuming a mask, persona, derives from the Latin "per" meaning "through," and "sona," "sound." The role we play to perpetuate our existence is presented primarily through sound. We create distinguishable characterological sounds as our instruments of manipulation, our attempts to get from and fend off the other person. Fritz is repeating "If the voice is phony, the whole personality is phony."

Immediately upon meeting a client we are offered a great deal of information about who he pretends to be and how he imagines his world to be. If we hear fairly continuously a message of sound which is a cry, plea, seducing, bullying, or lecturing, we suspect that the client has given up much of himself, and we may have little to work with. But what we do have is the foreground phenomenon which this person creates, and our critical tool, his voice. We have the instrument and the bearer of his neurosis. If we fail to utilize this tool, the client remains trapped in his role-playing. He continues to call out to the world with the sound which obscures and defeats him, and the world responds accordingly.

Fritz makes the point especially in relation to the client who plays dead. "If the patient's voice is dead, he is (emotionally) dead." Regardless of what he says and of how he imagines that he is working in the therapy situation, as long as the client's voice is without life, he is not vitally present and he produces nothing of himself. If the therapist gets caught up in and responds to content and he ignores the message of the sound, the patient is denied access to his major obstruction. We must assume that he may come to us largely unaware of his message to others that he is not vitally alive and present.

Hear the client. Let him tell you through the quality of his sound of his message and his demand. Does he entice, applaud, demur, lull, insist, proclaim, deaden, devour, entertain, ridicule, invoke, threaten, soothe, apologize, plead, push, conspire? What does he *do* with his sound? And hear his rhythm, inflection, hesitation and choking, his flow. Hear his sound when he encounters frustration. At the appearance of an obstacle, the client has a good chance to play his special form of helpless, his own variety of the victim of circumstances not of his making. The therapist has a good chance to hear the appeal which the patient makes beyond words, as he tells the world with sound who he pretends to be. Fritz has written some eloquent verse setting forth some "sound relationships" with patients.[12] Read it for information and entertainment.

As we put aside words and ideational content to hear the client's sound as his message, we can begin to work directly with his phony personality; his persona. The role of the therapist now is to facilitate two processes for the client: his hearing of himself and his discovering how he uses this sound. Ask him to hear himself; what does he hear himself do? Ask him to utter gibberish rather than words, so that he comes to perceive the essence of his sound. Closing our eyes and experiencing ourselves blindfolded helps to put energy into our ears. Even familiar sounds then become fresh and clear. If he has trouble hearing himself, have the client first be with himself, allowing awareness of his body and emotions, and then return to listening. Experiencing the flow of ourselves energizes our perceiving. When he is willing to hear his own sound, the client is ready to begin to work with his voice as his primary devise for producing a characterization. Ask him to become his voice. Maybe he begins by describing rather than being. Give him then a situation in which he can experience himself as what he has described. Identify the role his voice creates. Improvise a situational drama for his playing out his role with others. Let him play his role at times using only sound, rather than words which distract. Or ask him to create a dialogue, playing his voice and its opposite. This work has the advantages of expanding his opportunity to create his own sound deliberately as he returns to become his voice after playing the alien sound, and of presenting him with the chance to re-own the lost part of himself inherent in the opposite role. For instance, in the case of the man who plays exhausted and dead and dreams of Groucho Marx, the laughter and joy he has given up are available to him in the character of Groucho. The woman whose voice assaults; is aggressive and tough, can become tender and yielding; the pleader gets to command; the preacher can become the searcher. The client gets involved in playing his voice's opposite often spontaneously and with joy. When someone seems stuck, failing either to hear himself or to experience himself as the sound he communicates, sometimes he gets through the impasse if I echo back or mimic his sound, or if I respond to him using the voice of the complementary role. At this point I am not so much facilitating as involved in playing an active role with the patient. If he whimpers and will not hear himself, I can respond as the comfortor, exaggerated. If he bullies and will not hear, I can respond subservient and cowering. Usually he gets the message, and we can go on.

## Dreams

Fritz looks at dreaming and sees "the most spontaneous of our creations" available to us. The dream presents the production of our own making which is the least cluttered with denials and the clearest expression of our existence. For distinguishing existence and problems of existence from symptoms, for finding life to supplant emptiness, and for resolution of existential difficulties, work with dreams. Gestalt theory asserts that our life script is complete in each of our dreams. The dream is a statement which brings the message of the composition of our existence. Consistent unremembered dreaming tells us that we refuse to face the issue and the problems of our existence. For the period of time of the client's remembering his dream, it reveals process which is unresolved. Once I heard Fritz say that a dream remains relevant working material at least for a year.

Working with dreams is one way to go, especially with the client who appears emotionally dead, and so provides next to nothing with which to work. Fritz reminds us that the person who seems to have given up almost all of his real self has usually a little vitality left, and this we can find in his dreams. Over and over the worth of dream work is re-affirmed for me as I work with people who are characteristically passive and who continuously report themselves to be unfeeling.

Gestalt theory submits that each character and object in the dream is a disowned part of the dreamer's personality. The basic method of working then has the client becoming each of these repudiated parts of himself. We include in the projections to be experienced and owned again any and all items—person, place, and thing—provided by the dream, however inconsequential a status the dream may seem to afford them.

In working with dreams, pay attention to the client's first statement. Usually at the beginning he provides the setting. "I am in a theater." For this person, life is a theater. We have already a huge clue about how this human being finds his being in the world. Recognize from the first how the client relates as he begins with his dream. Is he in touch with someone? If not, have him emphasize and exaggerate his autistic behavior. Encourage him to go more deeply into himself. Then ask him to return to the group and to relational behavior. Where does this person want to be with his dream? What happens when he leaves some aspect of it and returns to the present?

I am remembering Fritz's dream work with Sam. As he goes back and forth between himself and contact with the group, Fritz attends to Sam's inner experience, and Sam becomes aware that as he sees people, he "stops breathing." This is his first relating of his body process and being with people. Sam dreams of a demon who threatens his genitals, and he discovers now that just as he begins to allow some consciousness of his sensations, he brings in the demon who appropriates his attention. Fritz appears to focus on the timing of the dragon's appearance, and Sam knows now that, phobic in relation to his own feelings, he prefers to deal with this production of his imagination. Life is coping with dragons.

Facilitate the client's emotional becoming rather than his getting caught up in the DMZ process of reporting, by having him dramatize and exaggerate the roles of his dream. First, ask him to relive his dream, maintaining involvement by staying in the present tense. Encourage his continuing to "become," through encounters between the characters and the inanimate properties of the story and through his creating additional script. Since dreams are interrupted by our waking up often at the critical existential moment, it is worthwhile to ask the client to continue the story. Dream work provides a compelling stage for the spontaneous stirring of poignant feeling as the story of one's existence is laid bare, as well as for the emergence of self-torture modes as the client engages in dialogue between his contradictory, seemingly inconsistent parts. Begin with a dream, or a scrap of a dream, and the client begins to allow himself to remember others. Then the tale of his existence speaks undeniably through this series of his least edited productions.

Discover what the dream attempts to avoid. The event which can't be allowed is sometimes apparent as we look at the point at which the person wakes up. Often what is being avoided is suffocation or death. Sometimes sex. The client discovers through his dream that he operates on the basis of his own private equation: "If this occurs, then that will happen." "If I allow myself to know my feelings under these circumstances, I will become nothing." Over and over again in dreams, in therapy, in our existences, this statement occurs. We see clearly then the imagined threat upon which an existence is built. Once the client exposes the imagined unbearable, he has available to him the option of giving up his avoidance and risking the experience. Now, if he is willing to remove his private equation from its status of controlling his life, his existence can change. The confines of his existence need no longer deny him his life.

Let's look at Richard's dream. His dream is a journey into the conflict between his emotional being and his active self, to the impasse of his existence. We see Richard's right-left split as his motor, aggressive, coping side opposes his sensitive, perceptive self, and these parts of him are represented clearly on his right and on his left. The dream brings a direct and effective means of working toward realization of Richard's latent assertiveness, toward more balance between his sensing and acting abilities, toward resolution of his existential problem of physical inhibition.

Richard dreams: "I am in a dark room. There is a window on the left, a piano on the right. When the piano goes up, the window goes down, and vice versa." He pushes the piano up, exposing a view of beach and ocean; he pushes the piano down, and he sees a garden. Richard prefers the ocean view and rejects the garden. He pushes the piano up, seeking the ocean view again, "and the piano squashes. I squash, too. The piano and I squash out, across and flat. I can't breathe. I wake up. I am crying out."

I ask him to dream his dream again, and this time to continue his story, allowing it to go where it will. Again he stops the dream at the point where he imagines that he is helpless and unable to breathe, unwilling to go on through the impasse of his imagined suffocation. I ask him to create a dialogue, playing the roles of the window and the piano. Richard plays the window, detached and unresponsive. He says to the piano: "I don't see how we are related. I have nothing to say to you. I'm fine." He becomes the piano, agitated and full of rage, his violence directed at the window. Finally he seizes a pillow, hurling it over and over at the empty chair upon which he imagines the window, until at last he succeeds in knocking over the chair. And so Richard begins to energize his aggressive being. Through the role of the piano on the right, he is willing to become his rage and to fight his battle. I have not seen him willing until now.

The dream appears an elegant, economical, and clear statement of Richard's existence. He finds himself in a dark room; the dark room of his existence. In addition, only the necessary figures exist. On his left, or passive side, is a window. This is Richard's preferred side and the self he trusts, his sensitive, perceptive, receiving being. To the right, his active side, is the heavy piano which he cannot master, and which controls his access to and bars him from what he wants. "If I lift the piano to see (attempt to act to get what I want), I suffocate." I am hearing Fritz saying, as he did so often at the ending of sessions of dream work, "Do you get the existential message?" Richard discovers through his dream how he threatens himself with catastrophe in order to avoid asserting himself. His dream brings a way toward integration and centering and balance through his willingness to know and to work with the imagined catastrophe which he uses to perpetuate his existence.


# Organismic Self Regulation

Ronald Laing points out that until recently we had no way of referring to the person-in-his-world.[13] No word in our language suggested a human being together with others in a characteristic way. Recently, existential thought has attempted to describe that inherent quality of relatedness which is our being-in-the-world, our existence. Existential phenomenology offers a way of attending and of attempting to apprehend the unique way of a human being's experiencing of himself-among-others. Within this context which understands relatedness as a condition of being, Laing refers to the ideal of "understanding a patient's disorganization as a failure to achieve a specifically personal form of unity."[14] In the terms of Fritz's constructs, the "personal" has been more and more given up until little remains of the self. In the case of neurosis, whatever organization or form of unity exists, is relatively without the "personal." Gestalt therapy is concerned with the process of loss of awareness which occurs not in isolation but as we encounter other human beings under circumstances of stress. Through this progressive elimination of the personal which occurs as we block out outselves or others, we arrive at the composition and the terms of our existences. The process of Gestalt therapy reveals the patient from moment to moment as he engages in the function of denying parts of himself or avoiding his world, until through therapy he discovers unmistakably how he has evolved and now perpetuates a relatively fixed and repetitious mode of perceiving and of encountering others which specifically diminishes the personal. A "form of unity" exists, even if this "unity" consists largely of avoidance and looks superficially like disorganization. It is the crux or the essence of this "unity," the pattern of the person-within-world, which is the concern of the Gestalt therapist.

Let's note specifically Fritz's commitment to existential thinking, his concern with the nature of our being-in-the-world and with our taking responsibility for our existences, in relation to his concept of organismic self-regulation.

We have considered earlier various phenomena which are prevalent in the western world today, contained in shouldism and aboutism, which Fritz clarifies as antagonistic to and precluding any possibility of an existential approach. Shouldism expends energy to promote an image of what the person believes he ought to be, and aboutism utilizes our energy to avoid, primarily through intellectualization. In each case, what is disallowed are the simple experiences of perception of the succession of events around us as they are, and of response to those events from a being centered within his own process. In therapy we recognize the presence of shouldism and aboutism in order to eliminate these functions and to work toward the experience of "knowing" through the existence of an event, of understanding through being.

The statement of existential thinking that to know and to be are the same is implicit in Fritz's notion of organismic self-regulation, which primarily involves three phenomena: awareness, acceptance of what exists, and the emergence of the dominant need. If we put aside our obsessions with notions of what might be, and our responding out of evasion, we are left with the event of ourselves, the spontaneous process of our emotions and our bodies, happening among other events which include the others of our worlds. The person who truly regulates himself then first knows himself and others on the experiential level; he allows his being and theirs. Organismic self-regulation entrusts our well being to the guidance of an inner self which strives inherently toward health. The client who comes to take his clues from his physical and emotional being no longer creates continuous anxiety to assure the presence of a cloud between his intuitive process and his conscious knowing. His energy, freed from the struggles of moment-to-moment issues of survival-support, from the pulling in and pushing away of manipulative efforts, flows to assume the maintaining of his nurturance and is available for experiences which transcend the boundaries of himself experienced in isolation. The seeker in psychotherapy does not fulfill his quest if he fails to arrive at a point of giving up his self absorption; The self-transcendence of which Victor Frankl[15] and others speak as the goal of psychotherapy is surely an essential component of the Gestalt model of the healthy adult. Relying upon ourselves, our very soma, to provide intuitive guidance leaves our energy free to flow outward, beyond ourselves. We are available for the creative and committed involvement with the world which self-transcendence permits. In touch with the power that comes from being ourselves, we can accept without overwhelming anxiety and anguish the feeling experience which involvement brings.

# Conclusion

Fritz's legacy is complete. While he worked to the end of his life and hoped to achieve more which he had even then in process, the work he leaves is finished in that it provides a complete system. He has evolved a theoretical structure and the elaboration of this conceptual framework into a detailed clinical methodology.

Increasingly, numbers of therapists who practice now are indebted to Fritz. Not all acknowledge the debt and perhaps some are not explicitly aware that aspects of what they do originate in Gestalt therapy. Fritz's message of hope reaches now across the United States and Canada and to places all around the world. Who can assess the totality of his impact?

I suspect that as the work and power of other men and women bring new gifts to psychotherapy, Fritz's legacy will stand.

# Bibliography

1. Kierkegaard, S., *Fear and Trembling* and *The Sickness Unto Death* trans. Walter Lowrie (Garden City, New York, Doubleday & Company, Inc., 1954) p. 262.

2. Kopp, Sheldon B., *If You Meet the Buddha on the Road, Kill Him!* (Palo Alto, California, Science and Behavior Books, Inc. 1972) p. 2.

3. Perls, Frederick S., *Gestalt Therapy Verbatim* (Lafayette, California, Real People Press, 1969) p. 16.

4. Heer, Fredrich, *The Medieval World*, trans. Janet Sondheimer. (New York, New York, Praeger Publishers, 1969) p. 129.

5. Sartre, Jean-Paul, *Being and Nothingness*, trans. Hazel E. Barnes (Secaucus, New Jersey, The Citadel Press, 1974) pp. 91-92.

6. Perls, p. 19.

7. Ibid., p. 40.

8. Laing, R. D., *The Divided Self*, (Baltimore, Maryland, Penquin Books, 1972) p. 39.

9. Perls, p. 38.

10. Laing, R.D., *Self and Others,* (Baltimore, Maryland, Penquin Books, 1969) pp. 17-32.

11. Laing, R. D., *The Politics of Experience* (New York, New York, Ballantine Books, Inc., 1971) pp. 19-20.

12. Perls, Frederick S., *In and Out of the Garbage Pail,* (Lafayette, California, Real People Press, 1969).

13. Laing, R.D., *The Divided Self,* p. 19.

14. Ibid., p. 24.

15. Frankl, Victor E., *Man's Search for Meaning,* trans. Ilse Lasch. (New York, New York, Simon & Schuster, Inc., 1972).

## BOOK TWO

# Legacy from Fritz

(Lectures, Memories, and Transcripts)

*by* Fritz Perls

*"Come preach to others what you want.
You mean yourself and not the world."*

Fritz Perls

# Preface

*The Legacy from Fritz* is a special book for me. It represents in a small but unified way all of the three gifts that Fritz left to the psychotherapeutic community. His greatest legacy is that he gave those of us who have studied Gestalt therapy a new perspective about how to approach the practice and theoretical development of psychotherapeutic endeavors. He opened many windows and many doors to those of us in the people-helping professions about how to help ourselves and our clients to become self-supporting in coping with the world in a way that allows us to grow, mature, and expand our vast potentials in an exciting, vibrant, and ongoing way.

This book represents Fritz's legacy in three major ways. First, he left us his wisdom, his theoretical, and practical new ideas to organize our experience as therapists, which is included in "The Teaching." This is a series of mini-lectures he gave at Lake Cowichan in Canada. They form a concise presentation of his Gestalt theory, which has not until now been published and available for others from which to learn.

His second gift is his technique—present in this volume in the form of transcripts—transcripts which offer the widest variety of his work as a Gestalt therapist, from dream work to the treatment of stuttering; from the resolution of grief to his latest innovation; dream work with couples; from the days at Esalen to his last years at Lake Cowichan—all are present in this one volume, to be studied and learned from.

The last and probably the most important gift in Fritz's legacy is a generation of trained and practicing therapists, who in years to come will train others in his techniques, expand his theories and share the memories of a most unusual man. Indeed, one member of this generation has spoken out in the first book of this volume: *Gifts from Lake Cowichan* by Patricia Baumgardner, one of the many he trained at Lake Cowichan.

Loved and hated, laughed at and scorned, revered as a teacher, guru, and saint, he will not be forgotten. And neither will the wisdom of his theories, nor the power of his techniques.

May your work be known, Fritz, and learned, and used. I am grateful, and I thank you for your legacy.

Richard Bandler, *Editor*

## CHAPTER ONE

# The Teachings

## The Essence of Growth and Potential

I want to talk now about the essence of growth and potential. My definition of growing maturation is the transformation of environmental support to self-support. A baby needs all support from the environment. Then we learn to develop some potential to crawl, to communicate, to make some noises. Later on we learn to walk, to have friends, and so on, until we are relatively able to stand on our own two feet, and use our own resources instead of using the resources of the environment. Now each time we demand (whether directly or indirectly) environmental support, we create a dependency. Each time we refuse to use whatever there is in us, we lose a bit of our freedom.

Now, what happens if in the process of maturation as a child or growing adult we feel frustrated and cannot, or do not want to develop our own resources? Then there is an impasse. We do not get what we need to cope with the world, and so at that moment we develop character. We start role-playing, we start manipulation of the world. And according to the situation, we start manipulating the world by playing helpless, or playing bully, or we play stupid. Or we might play the patient and become sick to get the attention we need. But in every case we are not willing to invest ourselves and we are not willing to believe that we are capable. Now this is part of what we are doing in Gestalt therapy. When our patients come to us, they come to manipulate us into supplying the environmental support they have failed to secure in the world. We put them in a situation of frustration. And just as we consider every interpretation a mistake of the therapist, so, too, do we consider every other kind of helpfulness beyond an absolute minimum to be supplying the environmental support that prevents our patients from developing their own support; self-support.

So we all write our scripts—we play one kind of role to get some support and another kind of role to get some other kind of support. Thereby we are always hoping to be able to cope with life, but each time, as I said before, we refuse to use what's in us and seek environmental support, we lose a bit of freedom and we lose a bit of ourselves. Sometimes we are proud and don't want to demand support from the environment, so we play independent. Independence doesn't mean you are free, it means, at best, self-frustrating and self-torturing games. We had a beautiful case here with Ann. She wants some comfort and rest and she wouldn't ask for it or supply it. That's the difference between being able to be self-supportive in contrast with being independent.

So what kind of support do we demand from the outside or refuse to demand but still believe we do not have? What do we project as our needs, like the customers of a supermarket, when we go for therapy? In Gestalt therapy the best project screen in this respect is the therapist.

If a patient wants to be omnipotent, then he will see the therapist as omnipotent. If a patient needs to be loving, then he will see the therapist as capable of giving love. This is also what we as Gestalt therapists look for in the dream; what kind of support is demanded from the outside? Learning to identify with the different parts of a dream, and different parts you find in another person you will realize that you've got it in yourself.

All you need is there, you've got it in you! But you don't know it.

I wrote this poem about this a few years ago.*

Come, preach to others what you want.
You mean yourself and not the world.
For mirrors are, where you assume
You look through window's light and gloom.
You see yourself, you don't see us.
Project yourself, get rid of thee.
Impoverished self, take back your own,
Become the projection, play it deep.
The role of others is yourself.
Come, take it back and grow some more.
Assimilate what you disowned.

If you have hate for something there,
This is yourself, though hard to bear.
For you are I and I am thou.
You hate in me what you despise.
You hate yourself and think it's me.
Projects are the damndest things.
They fuck you up and make you blind.
Blow up to mountains little hills
To justify your prejudice.
Come to your senses. See it clear.
Observe what's real, not your thoughts.

Now, there is one more point to be considered. In order to get the environmental support you want, you have to be in control. You have to control the persons who give you this support. So the result is you become control-mad. You control yourself. You control other people. You believe that only if you're in control can you achieve the support you want. And you control yourself in order to create an image which does not fit reality, which means your inborn potential. The result is that we are growing up completely distorted—valuable parts of ourselves are eliminated, repressed, or projected. And other parts which haven't the support of our authentic personality are played. And this is called phony. We become phony by playing a part without the support of our real selves to get others to support us. So

*From *In and Out of the Garbage Pail* by Frederick S. Perls, © 1969 Real People Press.

you can imagine the kind of lopsided life most people live? A part is put on, another valuable part is repressed. So what's left? The hollow men of our time.

## Energy and Awareness

I would like to talk a bit about the most difficult thing in, let's call it psychotherapy—the *dynamic*. The energies provided by the organism, or by the universe for the organism and within the organism to be able to live and have all the experiences we potentially can and do have. The work done about this so far isn't very impressive. We have Freud's notion of cathexis and his playing around with the idea of libido, which if it were true would mean that only the sexual hormones would provide the energy for the living organism.

And we have the work of Bergson about the *elan vital*. But this is altogether very unsatisfactory. We really need a combination of a physicist and a biologist to get some understanding of this process. Now much of this is highly theoretical and not very interesting to the practitioner, but some of it is very important and will turn out to be useful. For instance, the dynamic of attention is very little understood. Yet if we are aware of something pleasant, it is easy to pay attention to it. In other words, it is easy to integrate our awareness and attention. This means to pay attention with our senses and assimilate what is available from the world with immediacy. But when we are aware of something unpleasant, then we become phobic, and one of the best means to avoid this is to *withdraw attention from it*; change the attention from the issue at stake to something else. The famous example is the husband who is lying in bed with his wife; he's not very excited, the awareness of his wife is not very pleasant, so she says to him, "Can't you think of anybody else *either?*"

But if we take the lesson from this as an antidote against phobia, we could learn that paying attention to that unpleasantness or painfulness will have its rewards. Suddenly the dynamic will take over and the unpleasantness, or painfulness will be transformed. The unpleasant will become pleasant as attention and awareness meet, and the integrative process begins and grooving begins.

Now, if we come back to physics and try to understand a bit about this dynamic in general, there are several things we can learn. One is that one form of energy can easily be transformed into another form of energy: the movement of a river into electricity, electricity into heat or light, etc. Chemistry shows infinite varieties of transformations of one kind of structure into something else.

I think we can assume that the same thing is taking place in the organism. To produce heat we have chemical processes and our nervous system uses electrical procedures to produce that peculiar phenomenon which we call awareness, which is probably something akin to the fluorescence of the television picture tube. But we do not know anything about the chemistry of awareness yet. I personally believe it is one of the three universals: extensions (spatial), durations (temporal), and awareness or knowing. There is something else you can learn from physics or chemistry. If two atoms come together, if they are interested in each other, if they have an affinity, a love for each other, then we realize that once they come together they need less support. So a lot of energy is freed in the process of their coming together. For instance, in the form of an explosion. If you join hydrogen and oxygen, energy is freed and what remains is water. We have water plus so-and-so much surplus energy. On the other hand, if we want to divorce these molecules again, we have to give them a lot of energy to let go of their mutual hanging on, to separate them, so they can provide their own capsule, so to speak, their own isolation barrier; their own ego barrier.

Now we find the same process again and again in human beings. We have molecules like habit formation, we have to use energy to split them apart. If an integration takes place, as you have in therapy sometimes, a lot of energy is suddenly freed and all kinds of explosions can take place in this process—explosions of joy, anger, grief, orgasm, or whatever.

Now the most interesting part of this process is what I

call a hole in a person; a sterile void. This seems to be the most difficult part of my work for people to understand.

A sterile void is the opposite of a fertile void. Let me explain this. As with most processes in Gertalt therapy, voids are polarities. On one end is the sterile void, experienced as nothing. On the other end is the fertile void; something is emerging. In this fertile void there is a nothing-ness, just process. The fertile void is our means of transforming confusion into clarity. It is our source of self-support. Now these holes which are the space for further development are usually experienced as nothingness, emptiness, or lostness. So we run away.

We experience tremendous dread when we experience nothingness. In our culture, nothingness is unconsciousness; for us it is emptiness equivalently. Nothingness in us is equal with nothing being there, being empty, being lost. So in order to avoid this emptiness we either fill in this hole artificially with all kinds of over-compensations, with verbiage, with symptoms, or we avoid it altogether and become autistic-catatonic.

We also create at the same time a fixation on our systems. The dread of the nothingness is so tremendous that we hang on desperately to what *is*. And the tragedy of this is that all the dynamic energy of the organism is now utilized in maintaining the status quo. When the dynamic energy in our organism goes into this avoiding behavior there is no energy to go into the hole and make the sterile void or hole into a creative void.

I believe all symptoms are a stagnation or condensation of energy or, as I call it, the excitement of the organism. Excitement is the psychological equivalent of excitation of the protoplasm. If you are able to pay attention to your excitement, to be aware and attend to that awareness of excitement in whatever form, then something begins to happen.

If you attend to the stagnation of excitement systems, then this foreground figure can again link up with the background and the excitement instead of being, let's say, hysterical. Or panic or dread can flow into the total organism as life supportive vitality. And the verbiage, or avoiding behavior of sorts can flow into intuitive response. In this, nothingness becomes the source of self-supportive behavior and this, in a nutshell, is the purpose of Gestalt therapy.

## The Process Approach versus The Thing Approach

Today I would like to contrast the "process approach" with the "thing approach." The "thing" has become a god that is the word; the nouns have become gods that make things, that do things. We say a *thought* is coming into my head. This is foolish, it is "as if" the *thought* were a thing that can come and go, and secondly "as if" it could come and go by its own choosing and move under its own power. "As if" the *thought*, my *head*, and *me* were all separate things, that make things and do things. Sounds silly, doesn't it? But as they say in the New Testament; In the beginning was the word and the word was God. This is how mankind started out to explain the world. Some god is doing things, making things. Today the noun, god, has new names: nature, gravity, electricity, and the electron. But at least noun names that we have given to the forces of nature don't stop us from knowing that electrons are not fixed, but are always in motion—moving particles perfectly relating to each other. So a thing is something that is frozen, fixed, that is substance, that is apparently touchable, and can only be moved because some other thing bumped into it, or pushed it, or stopped it from moving like a wall stops a rolling ball.

The word "now" also has this kind of fixation of process, and a damned difficult fixation at that. Because nobody can get hold of the "now." The very moment you try to get hold of it, it's gone. Now that the experience of "now" is gone, what happened? I would like to say something in relation to one of the most frequent projections of the neurotic, or, let's say, the autistic character; namely, his need for attention, for being looked at. This is in contrast to the healthy person who pays attention and invests his interest and energy in observing and coping with the world. And in this coping process where the attention and awareness come together there is the experience of the "now." But more important than this, is that the greater the intensity of the awareness of the "now" experience the greater are the chances of this process affecting the organism in a very special way. The greater the intensity of awareness the greater is the chance of a tracing.

In Gestalt therapy we call it a grooving process. This means there is an after-image that links up the past and the acquisition of experience. And this grooving always provides one part of the Gestalt: the background.

I like best the metaphor, (though it is not really a metaphor, but an example), the idea of listening to a symphony. While you are listening for a fraction of a second you are aware of the sound, but the traces build up the background to the sound, so you get acquainted with the whole symphony. Once we understand this we can fully concentrate on the experience of the now, the ongoing process of hearing sounds, seeing, observing, being with the other thing called the world and the immediacy of the experience will create the Gestalt, that figure and background that make up grooving. Sounds so easy, and it would be if it were not for our "DMZ."

You see you will not be able to do it as long as you are not immediately involved with the ongoing process and that is the great difficulty of becoming authentic, of being real, because between me, my experiences and the world we have, as I try to explain a big intermediate layer, this DMZ—a middle zone. This zone is full of verbiage, full of complexes, prejudices, catastrophic expectations, explanations, excuses, trying, yes, a tone of trying and trying to understand. And if our energies are taken up by those processes we cannot possibly be fully in touch with the world, which at the time means we cannot fully assimilate and understand the ongoing process. In other words, our tools for growth are interrupted; they are busy trying to make sure. But once we realize this we can use the tool, we can integrate attention and awareness. I would like to make another point here, which is that attention and awareness will not be integrated, will not get together for most people as soon as the awareness becomes unpleasant, painful, or uncomfortable. At that moment we will deny the experience, our attention goes into the DMZ and we start mind-fucking; we start being frightened. So no Gestalt can be closed, no grooving can take place, and the consequence of this is that no maturation can take place.

All these unpleasantnesses are part of our frustration blocks, part of our unwillingness to face the unpleasantness of closing obsolete *gestalten*, of working through the frustrating experience of coming to terms with the world, of relating outselves to the world. Instead we block ourselves in two main ways; first we interrupt with pre-associations, our expectations of the catastrophic, with our fantasies of internal verbiage. We avoid by going on sidetracks, having symptoms and second thoughts about our experience; we explain and make up excuses. But the result is always the same: we involve ourselves in our DMZ, instead of experiencing and using our ability for grooving, for growing and for coping with the world.

So this is what we are up to in Gestalt therapy—the integration of attention with intensified awareness. How is the process approach different from the thing approach? The name God has been applied to psychiatry. Freud devoted his whole life to prove to himself and others that repression of sex was bad and the cause of our problems.

The scientific approach during his time was that the problem was caused by something in the past like a billiard cue pushing billiard balls and the cue was the cause of the rolling balls. Of course, then, the problem was what pushed the cue, and so on and so on until we have God as the cause or some poor woman who ate an apple thousands of years ago. In the meantime, our scientific attitude has changed. We look to the world for processes, for systems, not cause-and-effect, stimulus-and-response. We look upon the world as a continuous ongoing process. Everything is in flux. We never step into the same river twice. In other words, we have made in time, (but unfortunately not yet in psychiatry) the transition from asking *why* to the process questions *what* and *how*.

In Freud's time, science, as did he, asked why? Scientists looked for reasons, causes, rationalizations. They thought that if they could change the cause they could change the effect.

In our electronic age we don't ask why anymore. We ask how. We investigate the structure—the molecular structure, genetic structure, chemical structure. And when we understand the structure then we can change the structure. And the structure we look for in Gestalt therapy, the structure we are most interested in, is the structure of our life script.

This is the structure of how we avoid the immediacy of experience. Life scripts are the structures of how we play games that we believe will be safe, but most of our life scripts are the structures of how we keep ourselves from being alive, in touch with the world, and able to cope.

## Pain and Pleasure

I want to talk about the basic biological, pschological phenomenon—pain and pleasure. There are many aspects of satisfaction, dissatisfaction, being high or low and so on. Nature has created pain in order to draw attention to the pain. If we disregard the painfulness, let's say, in an organ, and override it, we are likely to do real damage to the organism. If I have a broken leg and I want to walk with it, the pain indicates, no, keep still in that case. So the biological pleasure pain principle is valid.

Now we also experience pain and pleasure in our fantasy. Somebody calls you a son of a bitch, it's unpleasant to you, you experience this as being hurt. Now there is no end to this: I am ashamed, it's an unpleasant experience, painful; I feel proud—it's pleasant. Now if a person, and this varies trmendously, is aware of himself and of the world he experiences pleasantness, indifference, or pain-un-pleasantness. Now invariably we find that most people are not willing to experience unpleasantness on the fantasy level. They equate this with unpleasantness on the reality level. And at that moment when we face something un-pleasant we become phobic. This is the decisive point, without which we will never be able to understand the psychopathology, growth process, and so on. At that moment you are running away, you avoid going through hell or whatever the unpleasantness is. With this phobic attitude, we cannot come to closure of the gestalt, cannot finish the business at hand. And these fantasies that this is unpleasant, that something catastrophic will happen, is so much taken for reality that we always find means and ways again to dodge the issue.

This is the task of the therapist—to show where the patient becomes phobic, where he cannot accept the phenomena of unpleasantness. In spite of having experience even in therapy, in good therapy, a thousand times, that by staying with the unpleasantness it invariably changes into pleasantness. Each time you face again some unpleasantness in fantasy, you run away. If a person dreams that he's been eaten up by a lion, he takes this for reality and is not willing to be eaten up by a lion, although his rational mind can say that he can be eaten up a thousand times; he's still alive. You can kill a person a thousand times in fantasy; the person is *still* there.

In other words, again, the differentiation between reality and fantasy is the decisive issue. Craziness is always in the head, as they say.

Now we started out the first session with the fact that all knowledge comes through awareness, and awareness is always taking place in the here and now. And if we stay with what is called in Gestalt therapy the *awareness continuum*, we find that the patient will interrupt the awareness continuum as soon as he meets something unpleasant. And then he either runs to a position of support or he withdraws altogether, he might start mind-fucking, explaining; he might start his role playing, poor me, games, become melodramatic, become clever, abusive, depressed, all kinds of gimmicks in order to avoid the simple encounter with the unpleasant.

# Gestalt Formation

I want to talk today about the Gestalt formation—the biological Gestalt formation. I have said before that awareness is differentiating self-awareness from world-awareness. Now, if we are only aware of ourselves, then we live in a vacuum; we are autistic. We would have needs like hunger and thirst, but would have no resources to get those needs filled. We would be unable to tell the difference between water and fantasized water. If we had awareness of only the world we could detect water, but wouldn't know when we were thirsty, or when we were satiated. In either case, we would die. So there is always the need for a complete and over-all total experience of self and otherness. And I deliberately say "otherness" instead of "world." When we talk about the self in modern humanistic psychology we go into Maslow's trap and write self with a capital S. We then retrieve the superstition that the self is soul, or essence, or something precious, and not identification by the whole being. Then we fall back into the splitting syndrome of describing ourselves as bodies inhabited by ghosts, and the body is just a fragile shell in which the ghost lives for a short while. Self means contrast with otherness, so when I say "do it myself," I am, in fact, saying, "no other is doing it." If I attack myself, it means I don't attack somebody else; I attack myself which is a nonsense description. I am really describing the systems that occur when I interrupt my own immediacy and don't attack the other. Instead, I use up the excitement of my organism—I use my energies to create systems. So in healthy organisms there is a relationship between the self and the world, and the relationship is a Gestalt. When I wrote *Ego Hunger and Aggression* in 1947, people who even bothered to read the book were outraged that I debunked the whole instinct theory. Where the instinct was located nobody knew. So I introduced the theory of the organismic balance. We don't have organisms—we *are* organisms. And as an organism (like any other organism—plant or animal) we have a number of very subtle systems built in. Each system has what I call a zero point of optimal functioning. For instance, the thyroid gland has to produce a certain amount of thyro toxin with other chemicals. If it produces too much, we have over-excitement—over-anxiousness. If we have too little, we have the mongoloid type—sluggishness, lack of intelligence and so on. Now, this point of balance is the optimum functioning point of this system. Our fluid levels, such as water, also have this zero point. If we have too much water in our systems, we are bloated. If we have too little, we are dehydrated. This balance point must be maintained or our chemical processes of metabolism will not work. Now, each time the organism is thrown out of balance, or leaves the optimum zero point, the surplus or acquisition of the minus supply must be gotten rid of. And this is where the peculiar Gestalt formation takes place. If it's too hot and you sweat, you lose water and dehydrate the self. The self has a minus of water, so automatically the self concerns itself with water. Suddenly only things concerned with water will emerge in the world. We have the signal of thirst, and as soon as the signal of thirst appears, there suddenly appears a water tap, or beer, or whatever is required to restore balance to the organism. A mailbox doesn't enter your awareness until you need to post a letter, and then suddenly a mailbox appears. A man can walk down a bumpy road—let's say the road to him is not bumpy. But if he drives a car down this road, suddenly he'll discover the bumps, of which as a pedestrian he was not aware. So both the organism and its environment enter the foreground as a function of emerging needs of the organism in the environment. Once satisfaction is achieved, the foreground need then recedes into the background of awareness. And the next important need, urge, or want will come into the foreground of our awareness. So nature is a kind of self-controlling system; very subtle, tremendously sensitive to its needs. The very moment we interfere, that we superimpose artificial social controls upon the system, it will be out of kilter. Any self-control will damage the whole organism as soon as it is in conflict with a basic and vital need. Any time we gain a victory over ourselves, we inflict a tremendous defeat upon ourselves. And if we go so far, and this is very frequently the case, as to control feelings which have to meet social demands or ideological demands (our ideals) when we start to desensitize these feelings, we get out of touch with what needs go with what feelings. The result is that no rectification can take place. This is similar to certain neurological cases where some nerves are damaged so there is no longer any sensitivity. You lose your detection temperature, so you get burned and hurt because you are not aware of what is going on. And we are all so miraculously adequately built for this Gestalt process. We have two systems built into the organism with which we relate to the world: the one system is the sensory system, the system of awareness, or orientation, of sensing and knowing, and the other the motoric system, the system of doing, of coping, of moving in the world. The most interesting phenomenon here is that whenever an urgent need emerges, there is an unbelievable cooperation of the whole organism. If I am thirsty, it is not just the dehydrated tissues that to to the bottle of water. Thirst takes command of my total organism and then I go with my resources, both sensory and motoric. I mobilize whatever resources I need to return my organism to balance. I slake my thirst by unified sensing and acting, then thirst recedes into the background, and a new foreground emerges in a never ending stream of awareness. If this system is disturbed, we lose faith in nature. We start to make sure that our needs are fulfilled—we fill our larders, we have a thousand lovers, we have stores of water, we take out insurance policies. Then we begin to desensitize and we lose confidence that we can manage without having already made sure. We develop a character as a means to manipulate the world to do things for us; to make sure for us. And as this making sure, this self-control interrupts our natural process of Gestalt formation, we go further out of kilter. The moment you lose faith in the functioning of the organism, you find faith somewhere else—in religion, philosophy, or psychotherapy. It is so difficult to realize that we cannot be different from what we are, and that if we let be, the organism has all the power and all the intuitive potential to rectify itself. What's more, if we do not trust the functioning of the organism (self-regulation), then we try to apprehend the future—we jump out of the functioning of the organism and go into the future. The gap between the now and the future is called anxiety. As you probably know, anxiety is one of the most important symptoms in psychiatry. One of the differences between Gestalt and other forms of therapy is that we do not fear anxiety states and try to eliminate them, but rather consider them valuable symptoms because anxiety is the bottled up life force of the organism. Anxiety is excitement. If you look upon anxiety as a symptom of jumping into the future, then you can retrieve a great deal more of the life force that has stagnated. If we invest our life force in making sure of the future, and the main activity of securing the future is our fantasy, we create a great gap in ourselves. We cannot possibly see the future as we walk blindly backwards into the future. By "blindly" I mean that we see only the past, and as we live in fantasy of the future, we cannot see the now, so we see only the past. So we have to fill in the gap of this lacking view, and we do this with planning, apprehension, catastrophic expectations, anastrophic expectation and so on. So we're always busy-busy-busy-busy-busy escaping reality, escaping the present, escaping the possibility of regaining our balance, and of developing our own potential.

## How I Manipulate the World*

*Introduction by Carl Humiston*

Gestalt therapy is the name that Fritz Perls applied to his method of psychotherapy. Whenever he talked about Gestalt therapy he loved to talk about responsibility. One of the main aims of Gestalt therapy was getting a person to take responsibility for himself; for his own life, to achieve self-support.

He talked in this film about how so many of us will find ways of placing responsibility on others, of avoiding taking responsibility for our own lives.

My example would be guilt. You see, in order to feel guilty or think guilty we must see that we have failed to live up to someone else's expectations, failed to live up to

* Aquarian Productions, Ltd.

something that is out there, rather than taking responsibility for ourselves. Also in this film he demonstrates with a group exercise one of his most powerful methods—getting a person to own his own behavior.

Sometimes Fritz would even tell a person to brag about doing something which the person himself regarded as bad or undesirable or even hated to admit that he was doing. Whenever a person owns his behavior: "I did it, and I did it well" two things happen. One is that the energy that had been tied up in that behavior becomes available to flow into the rest of the person's life the rest of his activities. The second thing that happens is that his behavior begins to change, by itself, spontaneously and without further effort.

————◇————

I want to talk a bit more about the growth process. The key word here is responsibility. Responsibility means the ability to respond, which is often distorted into obligation.

An obligation is an action which one undertakes under the pressure of a "top dog"—whether or not it's an inner or outer top dog. And any obligation is usually accompanied by resentment. Responsibility means "I'm sensitive," I'm capable of responding. I know what's going on. And as I'm only aware of what I am experiencing and how I see the world, I can only be responsible for myself and for nobody else. And, of course, there are very many people who love dependency and want to push the responsibility onto somebody else——such as, I want to be taken care of; I want you to direct me. People do it essentially to have a scapegoat. So if you tell me what to do, you are responsible. I can blame you if something goes wrong. And in contrast to taking responsibility is manipulation. I'm not taking responsibility for doing and producing what I want in my existence. I want you to do this for me. I manipulate you, by whatever means I have, to make you my slave, mother, or whoever.

I want you to be within my life script. I want to make a little attempt to see how much honesty we can mobilize in this group. Let each one of you tell the group how he or she manipulates the world. We have, for instance, subtle ways of manipulation, like a negative attitude: I resist you. I manipulate so that you can run your head against the stone wall.

Very famous manipulators are the bear trappers.

I suck you in with innocuous questions or with charm and wait for you to make the wrong move so that I can chop off your head. Or the Mona Lisa smilers; they smile and smile and nothing penetrates. Some people think "There's an idiot, I know better." A very good manipulator is the driver-crazy. All he wants to do is to drive you crazy and drive himself crazy. Another killer is the toxic person. Chicken soup is poison. You know, the Jewish mother who poisons you with her chicken soup? She makes you feel guilty and feel like such a bad person that you don't eat a well prepared meal. All those are ways to manipulate the world.

Now I would like you, each one of you, now to tell the group how you manipulate the world. You can do it by ingratiating yourself, playing crybaby, playing tragedy queen, or whatever.

*Claire:*  I say I'm not good enough.

*Fritz:*  This is one of the famous tragedy queen plays. If you only depress yourself enough then the whole world will get depressed: we call them the gloom castles, the crepe hangers, the melancholic people. They start gloom casting; if everybody else is depressed then they go away.

*Mark:*  I think I manipulate the world by criticism. By criticizing.

*Fritz:*  By criticizing?

*Mark:*  Right. And presuming that there is a better way to do things. And perhaps my way is the better way. That's what I would probably suggest.

*Fritz:*  In other words, by making other people inferior.

*Mark:*  Yes.

*Fritz:*  These depressing games play a tremendous part in this, our social context. Not only do we depress ourselves, but many sports, for instance, and many business deals are meant to depress the other person. If I win my tennis game, then you feel depressed. Some people go to such extremes that they are real killers. They have nothing else in mind than to make themselves feel better and superior. The same goes for business deals. The rationale is forgotten as long as I get the better of the customer.

*John:* I manipulate the world by having accidents.
*Fritz:* What's the purpose of that?
*John:* I let someone else take care of me.
*Fritz:* Yes.

*Jane:* I manipulate the world by always trying to hide what I'm feeling and yet still expecting people to understand. Outside of the smile, I like to imply a threat, possibly a physical violence if I don't get my way.

*Fritz:* That is close also to a very famous way of manipulating called blackmail. "If you don't love me, then—." Parents are great at manipulating their children through blackmail. They're famous all over the world for this. If you don't do what I want I call you bad and naughty, you don't get supper and get bad marks.

*Madleine:* I manipulate the world by *doing,* not feeling superior, but doing all I can, all I can possibly think of, being, being the most open I can, which is not good, because afterward, if somebody still doesn't come back, I say I did all I could.

*Fritz:* Or play innocent, yes?
*Madeleine:* Yes.

*Gordon:* I manipulate the world by waiting for situations to arise and then pretend I have the answers.

*Fritz:* In one respect I see that you understand role-playing, but not quite the intentionality of role-playing. What do you achieve by that?

*Gordon:* A sense of adequacy or even superiority.
*Fritz:* Yes, and maybe impressing people?
*Gordon:* Yes.
*Fritz:* Look what a great guy I am!

*Ann:* I manipulate the world by being more confused and lost and doing things in a way that demands intervention or criticism, so that I have people put me down or tell me what to do, and so that I'm not responsible then.

*Fritz:* In other words, by playing helpless.
*Ann:* Yes.
*Fritz:* Waiting for the knight in shiny armor.
*Ann:* Yes.

*Jim:* I manipulate the world by criticizing, and then if that doesn't work, then I demand, and if that doesn't work I throw a tantrum. I rebel, totally. And all of this is designed to place me in a superior position—a position of superior awareness, superior knowledge, and also, it's a step up to create obligations to me.

*Alan:* I manipulate the world by being helpless and withdrawing, and I draw other's attention to me that way.

*Toni:* I manipulate the world by waiting; waiting for people to make what I consider a mistake and then move in and show that I can do it better than they can or I know the way.

*Fred:* I manipulate by being passive and getting people to come to me.

*Ted:* I manipulate by sulking and not doing things right when I know I can. But if somebody helps me, then I say I know how to do it, but I don't have to do it alone.

*Ellen:* I manipulate the world by retreating when things don't suit me—sometimes in a depression but sometimes just being away, an escape.

*Georgine:* I manipulate people by pretending to focus on them, making them feel what I feel or want what I want. Taking pressure off me by putting it on them.


## Fantasy and Projection

We have two types of processes, the public one and the private one. The private one is usually our fantasy life; the public one would be variable behavior. So our fantasy is our private life. We have been talking about retarded children when we realized that we are all retarded ourselves, every time we don't behave immediately. If we don't respond to the situation at hand—externally or internally—but rather arrest our immediate response, then we falsify our way of being.

Many proverbs say this: "Think before you act," or "Look before you leap." To be immediate is too risky. Whether this risk is real or 99 per cent imaginary, born of our insecurity, the result is still the same. We lose more and more of our center, more and more of our ability to respond immediately with all our wits and potential. We delay our responses verbally when we rehearse, by computing, making sure, and finding out. This is a vicious circle. It starts when the excitement that is supposed to go into an immediate action (such as anxiety) is interpreted as fear and the excitement goes into "rehearsing" until often nothing is left but catastrophic expectations, and making sure with compulsive behavior in a situation that has 400 possibilities.

You make sure you cover 399 possibilities, and you miss the real one. That is the tragedy of making sure. You will always leave out what is really required when covering all the possibilities. In covering all the possibilities we are blind to the real thing. This is a very interesting paradox because the real thing is immediacy.

We have an "organ" called intuition which we have learned to mistrust. This intuition is the only true direction we have. I would say this is about the saddest plight of man: he has to make sure of so-and-so and thus misses what is obvious.

I will give you a social example. It's obvious, let's say, to a sane person that to go to the moon is an insane procedure. Now the establishment goes further in producing all kinds of safeguards for astronauts (twenty-one days of quarantine to protect these two, three, maybe four men who have very, very precious lives). At the same time, while the lives of these two or three or four people are becoming too precious, another situation exists like the war in Vietnam, in which the lives of the people from the same country become expendable. This whole insane procedure is covered up by all kinds of systems and other procedures. This is exactly how most of us live most of our lives—with the loss of reality.

The loss of reality becomes in itself another reality. We take our fantasies as real; we take our rehearsals as real. When we fantasize that we are killing someone, we are just as afraid of admitting it as we are if the danger to this person were real; as if the life of that person would really be in danger.

So we come back to basic assumptions, Psychosis and insanity are states in which we take fantasy for reality. The difference is that there is no way to check out a fantasy other than acting it out. By trying it out and admitting to the fantasy

I see if it is real or just a fantasy. I am not saying that you shouldn't fantasize. I am not making another "should I or shouldn't I." I play my fantasies. I am aware they are fantasies. I play the comparing game and when I come to the point where I believe there is a relationship between fantasy and physical reality then I feel it click. This is the *"ah hah!"* Trusting this *ah hah* is trusting intuition.

When you mistake your fantasy for reality you cut out a lot of what is presently happening. So we falsify reality by using this process and fail to admit to our fantasy. We don't dare speak up to what is immediate, to call a scoundrel a scoundrel. We block ourselves with our catastrophic expectations: if we call the other person a scoundrel something bad will happen. So we go through all rehearsals and instead of calling the scoundrel a scoundrel we change the subject. But once we begin to see the possibility of relying on our intuition, we make a marvelous discovery: those expected dangers are at least 95 per cent nothing but our own projections.

We believe that we have windows, but actually we have only mirrors. We see ourselves with our mirrors. This is part of total autistic behavior which interrupts our immediate behavior and communication. So we become really caught in our own fantasies. We rehearse instead of cope. And what comes out of us is, at best, a stale, anemic image of the vast potential we could have. I would like to say more about having mirrors instead of windows.

## Projections

This process of projection is very difficult to understand. This might be a guide for you. If you project your *total* personality into an event, this can be an artistic experience, a discovery of another way of being. If you project a *part* of yourself on another person instead, that is a paranoid experience. The question is, do you project your total self or do you alienate part of yourself?

If you alienate a disliked part of yourself—if you have been forbidding yourself to nag another person, for example, you keep yourself from being a whole person, by disowning this ability to nag. You say, "I am not a nagger." So nagger is then outside. "I am not like this other person who is a nagger." The nag is outside, or so it seems, and it looks back on you. But that part of yourself wants to come home, and you want to take it back, so there is a conflict.

This is a difficult concept to understand in Gestalt therapy, because now the character of projection changes. If somebody says to me, "I am afraid of you," I say, "so attack me." I see that this person must have projected his aggression onto me. The aggression exists but not in me. It exists in the mirrors of the other person, which he uses to experience his aggression as turned back on himself. His aggression is not turning on me, so that his feeling changes into fear.

Now the same thing applies to the interpsychic struggle. We project certain acts in the same way within our systems and then we call it conscience or "top dog."

Freud once made a drawing where he showed that the superego gets its anger from what equals the unconscious. Now how is it possible that we don't see this as projection? If you use your senses there is no need for anything to come between. But once we have interrupted the immediacy of our observations instead of using our eyes we have holes.

If we project our eyes, we live in a permanent state of watching, of being observed, of being self-conscious. If our ears are projected, we live in a state where we have to talk and make people listen. So the tools by which we can discover the difference between projections and fantasies and reality are gone.

Let's just start again from the beginning. We are whole persons. As we grow up certain parts of our potentials are disowned; they are projected; they are alienated.

Now when we project we are still halfway sane. We are looking, of course, for a place to hang our hat. Even the severe paranoic will not project into a vacuum. He will find a mistake another has made and use it as a place to hang his projection. And he will blow it up into a tremendous insult so that he is justifying his projection.

When we wish to act and we falsify our way of being, rather than acknowledging our wish to act on the world, the process turns on us. Then, instead of beating up someone else we then beat up ourselves, and hang the shingle of the one who wants to do the beating up on the outside and live in fear of him. At that point in time we are living in fear of fantasy.

Most of you know how preoccupied I am with dreams. I have found that working with dreams is the best way of dealing with all fantasies. This is provided you know the trick of every patient, and this is the only danger of Gestalt therapy. If the psychiatrist wants childhood memories he gets those memories from the patient. If the psychiatrist wants problems, then the patient gives him problems. Fritz wants dreams, so you dangle your dreams in front of him.

You can always see whether a dream is genuine or whether it is a phony dream used to avoid coping with present situations. Apart from this, the dream is a script of a person's life. I believe that a dream consists of projections of ourselves. Every part of a dream is a projected part of our personality. In dreams we use avoidances. Avoidances are ways in which we avoid immediacy; avoidances are how we mistake fantasy for reality. And the circle goes on until you break it.

## CHAPTER TWO

# The Therapy

*I believe the dream is really the*
*royal road to intergation.*

—Fritz

## Dreams

### The Existential Messenger (Lecture on Dreams)

As in psychoanalysis, the mainstay in Gestalt therapy is the dream. We work around the dream even if a person claims he has no dreams. This, in my opinion, means people are not willing to face their existential problems. So we then have these people take the dreams as something that is around somewhere and we have them talk to the dream to find out their objections to remembering the dream. We all dream and we can all learn and grow from our dreams.

In my opinion, the dream is much more than wish fulfillment of an unfinished situation. To me, a dream is an existential message. It can lead to understanding one's life script, one's karma, one's destiny. And the beauty of this is that once we take responsibility for our life script, for our dreams, then we are capable of changing our lives.

As with neurosis, our life script is situated in our fantasy life. I can not emphasize this enough. Again and

again we forget that we are fantasizing, that we are imagining images, that we are making pictures and voices. The
difficulty is to understand that fantasy is a fantasy is a
fantasy. And the faith we have in this fantasy, the belief that
it is reality is the only stumbling block. *Maya* is the Indian
word for "everything is delusion," and I believe they included sensory awareness. Ecclesiastes says vanity of
vanities—all is vanity. Let's be on the safe side for the
moment and say all is delusion.

We know very well that while we are dreaming we take
the fantasy for reality. We take the most absurd situation as
real. We are not astonished if we change suddenly into
another animal or if we change into another person. While
we dream we take fantasy as reality and when we wake up
and we begin to see the absurdity, the irrationality of it, so
we can then forget that the reality in the dream *is* a reality—a
reality of much deeper significance than all our logic will
admit.

To use the dream to the fullest extent we can proceed
systematically, and see what happens when you get a
patient and he tells you a dream. He will usually give you an
auditory story of what happened the night before, or many
nights before. Nothing of the vividness of the aliveness of
the processes of the dream is retained.

The next step is to bring the dream back to life. In
Gestalt therapy we do this by a simple grammatical twist.
We ask our patient to tell us the dream in the present
tense—to describe his dream's experience as if it is occuring
here and now—as if his dream is his present reality. And if
we want to reinforce this process even further, so the patient
may connect his life script with his dream experience, we
have our patient intersperse the statement "and this is my
existence" after every sentence. So our clients may then
connect the messages of their dreams with their life script in
awareness. One will say, "I am swimming in the ocean, this
is my existence," or "I can't find a place to rest, this is my
existence." "I feel like I'm going to drown, this is my
existence." You see, we have become so conditioned in
psychoanalysis to interpret the dream, to look for associa-
tions, for events that might be repeated, that the idea that

this dream is a little episode which contains the essence of life script is difficult to accept.

So, as our patient uses the dream in the present tense we move to the third step. We make a story or play out of the dream. Our patient becomes the director, the cast, and all the props. He moves around and sets the stage, describing where everything and every person is. He then begins the drama of reidentification. We have patients play all parts of the dream, interacting with all other parts always speaking with the "I" for identification and in present tense to bring the drama to life. In this process we can watch them become more alive. They will defreeze themselves, as they reintegrate all the pieces of themselves that have been fractionalized in the process of being socialized.

The beauty of this is that no matter how dead your client may appear, even if he appears to be a double corpse, there is still some genuine life left, and that's the dream. To me, life script means that there is still hope; that there will still be life in the deadest looking person's dreams. It may be a fear, a desperate attempt to get something, a fight, but something in the dream will have life. And when we have this patient identify with this life he will then transform; something will begin to happen, something will click. He will link up with the present state. He will begin on his own to reidentify with the scattered bits and pieces of his personality, which had only been held together superficially by the expression "I." Then when the click comes, the dynamic, the *elan vital*, the life force that has been disowned and projected into others will begin to flow into his own center and he will begin to be himself again.

The patient, as well as any of you who work with your dreams in this way, will find that each time you take back a few bits and assimilate them and make yourself somewhat less split and scattered, you will not only look more alive but you will feel more alive.

I would like to take a moment to mention recurring nightmares. They are most important. I don't know if I mentioned this yet, but Freud's mistake about the death instinct in these repetitive dreams was, in my opinion, that he failed to see that a repetitive dream is the outcome of an incomplete Gestalt. The dream is an attempt again and again to solve a problem. If we are not willing to go through that impasse, then the dream has to be repeated. These dreams will show you the way to help your patients finish the situation. There is one aspect of this I would like to mention.

In dreams we find the holes in the personality. We find the person has no eyes, or has no soul; one has no genitals; another no legs to stand on. Whatever is missing in the dream is missing in this person's existence. The dream directly points out these avoidances to being whole.

To sum up this whole thing I can ask if we have alienated certain parts of ourselves, how do we undo this alienation?

The alienation is undone by reidentification. And here comes another item which is very difficult to understand in the beginning: the fact that the word "I" does not stand for the person. "I" is an identification process. Certain tribes don't have the word "I." They say, here is a child, a child hasn't got an "I" yet. A small child will say, "Fritz wants chocolate." Or "Fritz is big." The "I" is identification, not symbolic identification, but identification. This is me. If we refuse to identify with our parts, for instance, being a nag, and I say not I, we fragment ourselves and slowly utilize all dynamic energies until we appear to be a shell inhabited by a ghost. We call this process alienation, "I disown it." And by reidentifying, by playing and becoming the projected part, by being able to metamorphize yourself into that thing, that mood, you link up again, it clicks, suddenly, and there's an "Ah *hah*" experience; an insight.

Once you start to assimilate, you start growing, you integrate again the disowned parts. The dream is the best way to proceed. If you just learn a little bit about the "how" of reowning your projections it can bring you insight, happiness, joy, and most of all life force.

Then the energy begins to flow into new directions and the process of neurosis, of increasing alienation is stopped and put into reverse.

The remainder of the book is comprised of transcriptions from films of Fritz Perls. Sometimes he is
working in a group with different individuals on
the "hot seat." Sometimes he is working with an
individual.

## Nourishing and Negative Aspects
## of Personality*

*Sharon:* I have a dream that I had, and it's stuck with
me. It's a—it opens up.
*Fritz:* Talk to the dream.
*Sharon:* Talk to my dream?
*Fritz:* You heard me.
*Sharon:* Dream, you seem ridiculous. And you don't
make any sense.
*Fritz:* See how this fits, you are ridiculous with that
smile. It's what we saw the other day, this ridiculing. So, in
the dream, I am ridiculous. I am ridiculous. I am ridiculous. I
already know, I know I'm ridiculous. What are you blocking
right now?
*Sharon:* My heart coming out of my mouth. So I can
talk.
*Fritz:* Okay, close, retreat in yourself. Get in touch
with yourself. Go away from us. What do you experience?
*Sharon:* I experience my body quivering and I see the
ocean splashing on my eyes. I feel like I'm getting bigger and
smaller.
*Fritz:* What do you see now? You came back to us, at
least, to the chair.
*Sharon:* (Sniffling) I see sparkly things.
*Fritz:* Okay, maybe you have a different dream now.
Tell us the dream in the present tense. Remember the four

* Media-Psych Corporation

stages. First, the story, which we can skip. Next, tell the dream in the present tense. Third step: become the stage director. Set the stage. The next step is to become and transform yourself into every little part of the dream.

*Sharon:* I'm in a strawberry, No, I'm in a milkshake factory and there's a great big machine that makes milkshakes and my mother appears next to me and she says, "I'll buy you a milkshake." And I say, "all right." So she buys me a milkshake and the big machine makes them, and she gets a chocolate one and I get a strawberry one. And she leaves because hers—she got hers first. So I wait and I get mine. Then I go, too. I guess it's a hospital; it's this place. (Laugh)

*Fritz:* What's so funny right now?

*Sharon:* It's not funny. (Sniffling.)

*Fritz:* Well, you were smirking.

*Sharon:* It's, uh, it's funny, but it's not funny. It's ridiculous.

*Fritz:* Say this to the hospital. Hospital, you're ridiculous.

*Sharon:* I will. I wasn't smirking at the hospital. I was smirking at what was coming next. Which was, I was going to the hospital to, uh, pick up my baby, which was—was ridiculous. And, it wasn't time yet. So I had to wait and I was, uh, walking around the hospital and there was all kinds of people there. And I was—

*Fritz:* Are you aware that you are slipping back into the past tense?

*Sharon:* (Sniffling) Yes.

*Fritz:* So go back to when you start to slip into the past.

*Sharon:* Um—I'd like a milkshake. I want a strawberry one. Now my mother's talking to me. She's not saying anything to me but she's talking to me. (Pause) I'll see you later. And now I get my milkshake.

*Fritz:* Your mother gets the strawberry milkshake?

*Sharon:* No, she gets the chocolate one.

*Fritz:* Chocolate one. And you get the—

*Sharon:* Strawberry.

*Fritz:* Okay, let the chocolate milkshake and the strawberry milkshake talk to each other.

*Sharon:* I'm strawberry and you're chocolate. I'm pink. And I taste sweet. But I—I have a different kind of sweetness than you do. My sweetness is, uh, it's real. It's, uh, it's not, um, uh, let's see. Well, I mean it, it tastes like a fruit. It tastes like something you could have besides.

*Fritz:* Please replace the it by I.

*Sharon:* Oh, I—I taste like a fruit that you could pick out of the ground. And, you, uh, I don't know where you come from. I'm a chocolate milkshake. I'm, uh, brown, I'm not brown, I'm, uh, kinda brown. Kinda milky brown. I, uh, taste rich. I have rich sweetness.

*Fritz:* What happens now?

*Sharon:* I think a strawberry milkshake is ridiculous.

*Fritz:* Say this to her.

*Sharon:* I think a strawberry milkshake is ridiculous.

*Fritz:* Say this to her.

*Sharon:* I think you're ridiculous.

*Fritz:* Say this again.

*Sharon:* I think you're ridiculous. I think you're ridiculous.

*Fritz:* Change seats. Say this to him.

*Sharon:* I'm ridiculous to you but, to me I'm not really ridiculous. Because I taste good.

*Fritz:* Say this to each member of the group. I taste good.

*Sharon:* I taste good. I taste good. I taste good. I taste good, I taste good.

*Fritz:* What do you experience when you say this?

*Sharon:* I feel like a, I feel like I taste good.

*Fritz:* All right, let's pick out another scene. Let the milkshake factory and the hospital talk to each other.

*Sharon:* I'm a milkshake factory. And I, I make milkshakes for people to eat. (Laugh.)

*Fritz:* To whom are you talking?

*Sharon:* To the hospital.

*Fritz:* Say this to the hospital. You said that far. Really get it, send the message to the hospital.

*Sharon:* I, uh, I, uh, make milkshakes for people to eat and they're good, they're good milkshakes and, but sometimes they make people sick and that's part of the reason you're there and you help people to get well.

*Fritz:* So. Be the hospital.

*Sharon:* I'm all white inside. And I smell really horrible. And this place is, uh, some places smell really clean, if you don't stay too long. And we, I, have milkshakes in me, too. But, my, I, mine aren't as special as yours are because that's your specialty. My specialty is to, uh, help people to make them well.

*Fritz:* Okay, let's try a short-cut. Be yourself again. And tell each one of us, I make milkshakes, I give you milkshakes and you end up in the hospital and then I have to cure again. Something like that.

*Sharon:* I make milkshakes and, uh, this milkshake that I, that you get, makes you sick.

*Fritz:* You say, I make you sick?

*Sharon:* But that's your fault. I, but that's your fault because you, maybe you ate too much, but if you went to the hospital, I could help you. I'm, I give you milkshake, and, and it makes you sick. It shouldn't make you sick.

*Fritz:* Please replace each time it, by I.

*Sharon:* I shouldn't make you sick. You go to the hospital. And get better. But that can make you sick too, or, I can make you sick, too. I am a milkshake and you get sick from me, and so you go to the hospital to get better.

*Fritz:* Can you condense the whole thing into one simple thing? I am nourishment and poison at the same time.

*Sharon:* Yeah. I am nourishment and poison at the same time. I am poison and nourishment at the same time.

*Fritz:* Okay, close your eyes. And withdraw from here. What do you experience? Where do you go?

*Sharon:* I'm someplace where it's—there's nothing but red.

*Fritz:* Yeah.

*Sharon:* But it's not hot.

*Fritz:* Do you see the red?

*Sharon:* Yes.

*Fritz:* Can you describe the redness in more, greater detail? What kind of red is it? Any differentiation there?

*Sharon:* It's a, it's a hot, like fire red. Like an apple red.

*Fritz:*   Like what?

*Sharon:*   The color of an apple. Only hot, hot red apple.

*Fritz:*   Hot red apple. Apple. So put the hot red apple in that chair. Talk to it.

*Sharon:*   How come you're so red? Your red is so vibrant. It's so alive, but it's not a good apple. It's—it's ugly.

*Fritz:*   Be this apple. Say this to the—

*Sharon:*   I'm not, uh, really ugly and, uh, I'm not hot. I just look hot.

*Fritz:*   What do you experience when you say this?

*Sharon:*   I experience that nobody believes me.

*Fritz:*   What about yourself?

*Sharon:*   I believe it. I—I don't understand the hot, not hot. I don't understand what that is.

*Fritz:*   So, let's sum up. What's your conclusion about this little bit of work we did?

*Sharon:*   Um, my conclusion is that I—I'm ridiculous. I've always known that I was ridiculous, but, uh, no, that's an excuse. And that I'm not really ugly.

*Fritz:*   So. Tell each one very quickly, you're ridiculous if. In which way are we all ridiculous? Start with me. How am I ridiculous? Make aloud thinking.

*Sharon:*   I don't know you're ridiculous.

*Fritz:*   Good. Next one. Very quick.

*Sharon:*   I don't know how you're ridiculous.

*Fritz:*   Quickly, find something ridiculous.

*Sharon:*   I—I don't know.

*Fritz:*   You're the only ridiculous person in the world.

*Sharon:*   No.

*Frutz:*   Now, look around. Anybody here ridiculous?

*Sharon:*   No.

*Fritz:*   Say to Marty. Marty, you're ridiculous.

*Sharon:*   Marty, you're ridiculous.

*Fritz:*   Again.

*Sharon:*   Marty, you're ridiculous.

*Fritz:*   How is he ridiculous?

*Sharon:*   He's a liar.

*Fritz:*   And you are Snow White?

*Sharon:*   No.

*Fritz:*   No. The poison apple? Yes. I know two great

killers. I think I mentioned this already. One of the killers is the word "but." With the word but you can kill anything. Everything can be killed by but. And this is why we replace "but" with "and" in Gestalt therapy. The other way is to ridicule. To ridicule is to kill. Every caricaturist knows this and every politician knows this.


## Classroom Dream*

About twenty people are sitting in a circle in the workshop at Esalen Institute in Big Sur. Dr. Perls is sitting in the circle as well. Louise, a young dancer of about twenty-two is sitting next to Dr. Perls, in the hot seat. Mary, her dance teacher, is in the workshop also, sitting on the other side of the circle.

*Fritz:*   I like to use as the center in my actual work, dreams. To me, dreams are an existential message, not just a story—an unfinished situation. I would like to show the group what one can do with dreams. Switching back to an experience I had about half a year ago when we did something similar with a moviemaker who worked with a dream, and he took over the part of making a film out of the dream. A dream is a good script. Let's see whether you can help me to relate the dream into a much more meaningful experience than we usually attribute to dreams. Who has a dream and would like to work? (Louise raises her hand) Okay, can you come forward? Your name is—?

*Louise:*   Louise.

*Fritz:*   *Louise*

*Louise:*   (Takes hot seat next to Fritz) This is a dream I had a couple of weeks ago. I was sitting in classroom on a stool. Chairs were lined up in twos and for some reason I was sitting in the front row and there was some young girl next to me on my left side. As I was sitting there, the professor was going on with something which didn't interest me and I turned to the girl next to me and I said, "One of my teeth has fallen out," and she looks up—(She mimes picking a back tooth out of her jaw and letting it drop).

* Media-Psych Corporation

*Fritz:*   What did you do with your tooth right now? Did you pull it out and throw it away?

*Louise:*   I put it down.

*Fritz:*   Go on with the dream.

*Louise:*   She turned back and didn't seem very concerned about the fact I had lost a tooth. I was sitting there and more teeth started loosening, and I suddenly was upside down, sitting in the same chair, and all of my bottom teeth just kind of fell just like this (she mimes more teeth coming out) and they all came out or were hanging by very little threads and I was upside down. The blood—the bleeding from the teeth—it doesn't seem logical, but it was going back into my throat and made it very difficult to breathe and I couldn't breathe and I wanted to scream. I was screaming for some kind of help, Help!, to somebody—something like this—and I felt rather astonished that nobody responded to this very peculiar plight and nobody was doing anything about it but just kind of going on. And this girl, who had kind of remarked about the teeth which had been falling out for two days, didn't seem concerned. I woke up with this tremendous sensation of choking.

*Fritz:*   Now you have started a story and I would like you to make a play out of it. Will you get up? You are the stage director, and the whole thing is taking place in the present tense.

*Louise:*   (Standing up) I want my shoes off. (Takes them off) Can I ask other people to play other parts?

*Fritz:*   No. You are everything. Set the stage.

*Louise:*   (As she speaks, she is setting the stage in mime and enacting the dream) Can I use this one chair? (She slumps in the chair) Here I am. (Gestures in front of her.) There's a blackboard up here with a very big professor; I don't recall its specific qualities. The professor is standing turned around, with his back to me—to the class. For some reason, the chairs are lined up in rows of twos. There's another chair here (gestures next to her chair) and there's a girl—all I remember is dark hair—sitting over here. People are writing notes and looking rather bored, going on like this, and suddenly for some reason my tooth—one of my bottom teeth—is falling out, and I'm kind of used to that, it's okay, but I still don't like it. So I turn to the girl next to me and I say, as if remarking on something as insignificant as the sun shining or something like that—and say, "my tooth is falling out." And she turns back and says, "well this is the fifth one in two days, isn't it?" and goes back to writing. I'm feeling a little perturbed, and I go on and write and pay attention, but then I'm aware there isn't just one tooth that is falling out. And suddenly I'm upside down, like this, in the chair. (She is upside down in the chair) My teeth are falling out in the bottom row and I can't breathe (she mimes with her hands at her mouth, still upside down in the chair, head hanging down and feet over the back) All the blood and saliva and so forth goes back down inside and I'm choking, arrrgh, arrrgh, like that, and I want—I want help, and I don't know what to do.

*Fritz:* Stay with this prospect of drowning. The blood is streaming out—

*Louise:* (She screams and chokes, tears at her head and contracts upwards, still upside down.)

*Fritz:* Scream!

*Louise:* (Screams) HELP! (Silence, long sigh.)

*Fritz:* Just let it happen; just let it happen.

*Louise:* (Cries, still upside down, wracked in the chair, holding herself and sobbing, agonized. She subsides and is quiet, her ribs heaving.)

*Fritz:* Where are you now?

*Louise:* (Quiet, withdrawn voice) I feel like I'm out of it. Like I'm . . . not in the situation.

*Fritz:* Come back. What do you experience now?

*Louise:* (Righting herself in the chair) More of a relaxed feeling.

*Fritz:* Now, let's start over again. I want, this time, the professor to dream this dream. Be the professor.

*Louise:* Uh huh. You want him to dream the dream as if he were—

*Fritz:* No. Be the professor. I call this dream work à la Rashomon. Look, it means different people see the same event from their point of view. "I am a professor . . ." Describe exactly what kind of guy you are.

*Louise:* (Standing up, miming this scene with alive

gestures) Okay. I'm a professor—maybe in my early thirties, late twenties, dark hair, very neat, good looking, perhaps only about that tall—

*Fritz:* I notice you always look at me.

*Louise:* Yes.

*Fritz:* What do you want from me?

*Louise:* Approval, or that I'm doing the right thing.

*Fritz:* Say this to me.

*Louise:* I want to feel like you feel that I'm doing the right thing.

*Fritz:* Let the professor say this to the class.

*Louise:* You know, class, I really want to know from you that you really like what I'm doing and that you feel that what I'm doing—

*Fritz:* Just then you looked at Mary. (General laughter.)

*Louise:* I'm asking her the same questions that I was asking you.

*Fritz:* Can you experience some of the resistance in doing this? Can you tell this to Mary? That you have difficulty in asking for her approval.

*Louise:* (Crouches in front of Mary, looking at her) Mary, I can tell you, but I can almost hear myself saying it without feeling, that it's very difficult for me to ask for approval from you.

*Fritz:* Say it again.

*Louise:* Lookit, I want your approval and I need it.

*Fritz:* Say this to Mary.

*Louise:* Mary, I want your approval and I don't know how else to put it. And I feel like I'm not talking out of me and it's driving me buggy.

*Fritz:* Tell Mary, "Mary, I'm going to drive you buggy."

*Louise:* Mary, I'm going to drive you buggy.

*Fritz:* Again.

*Louise:* I'm going to drive you buggy, Mary.

*Fritz:* Now say again what you want from her.

*Louise:* I still want and need your approval.

*Fritz:* Okay. Now please put Mary in that chair (he indicates the empty chair in front of the hot seat) and develop your—You're Mary now. Give Louise your approval.

*Louise:* (Goes back and sits down in hot seat, playing Mary) Louise, you know that you do have my approval. I do approve of what you are.

*Fritz:* In detail.

*Louise:* (As Mary) I like the length and the strength of your body. There's some looseness, some quality of looseness in some of your movements which is individual to you and I respect it. I like it. (Coughs)

*Fritz:* Now what does Louise answer?

*Louise:* (As herself) I guess I just wanted you to say that. I needed to hear it from you.

*Fritz:* What does it do for you to hear?

*Louise:* Mary, I want to hug you. I will.

*Fritz:* Hug the Mary in the chair.

*Louise:* (Hugging the Mary in the chair, the imaginary Mary) Mary is hugging Louise back; that's all that needs to be said. What needs to be said can't be said in words so much.

*Fritz:* Now go back and be the professor.

*Louise:* The professor in the dream?

*Fritz:* Yah.

*Louise:* (Stands and imitates a professor, her body loose and sarcastic; there is general laughter) I've got a blackboard and chalk.

*Fritz:* Talk to the blackboard.

*Louise:* (Low voice as professor; precise, mincing pose) You're what I rely on, baby, 'cause when I can't look out that way, you're the only way I can look. (General laughter)

*Fritz:* Now play the blackboard. What does the blackboard answer?

*Louise:* (Loud voice) You shithead, what makes you think I'm alive? There's not a whole hell of a lot I can give you. If I had my choice, I'd make myself white so your goddamn chalk wouldn't even show up. (Laughter.)

*Fritz:* Now give the professor a voice. Have a conversation between the professor and the blackboard, as you had a conversation with Mary.

*Louise:* (Small voice) This is the professor, and he doesn't really speak very loud.

*Fritz:* I am . . .

*Louise:*   I am the professor and I don't speak very loud. I feel myself to be a little man. I wear a coat and a tie and a white shirt and a dark suit. Well-polished shoes, only one of them always comes untied. And I like my work terribly much. (Laughter)

*Fritz:*   Will you now dance this professor?

*Louise:*   I can act the professor.

*Fritz:*   Act the professor.

*Louise:*   I take this chalk off the chalk rail; there's a book in my left hand . . .

*Fritz:*   In your left hand is the book, in the right hand is the chalk. Stop here. Now we have a new conversation, and new encounter: the chalk and the book. They meet each other; they talk to each other. The chalk represents your right side and the book your left side.

*Louise:*   Okay. (She slides to the floor, on her side, legs together tight, arms at sides.) I'm the book. (Brings her hands in front with a tight, minimal opening between them) I'm opened up this much. Sometimes someone comes along and puts me partly over in this direction . . . but I don't feel like . . . That chalk, it's way over there. I can see . . .

*Fritz:*   Talk to it. "Chalk over there."

*Louise:*   Chalk, I can see you over there, and you're farther, farther away than I figured.

*Fritz:*   Now play the chalk.

*Louise:*   (Moves so she is facing the book's place; as chalk she is stretched out, big, with a strong voice) Look, I can write all over you.

*Fritz:*   Say it again.

*Louise:*   There's nothing you can do. I can write all over you, and there's nothing you can do to me.

*Fritz:*   Again.

*Louise:There's nothing you can do to me, book.*

*Fritz:*   Again.

*Louise:*   Book, you can't do one thing to me.

*Fritz:*   Be the book again.

*Louise:*   (As book, she slams herself shut.) Chalk, you're wrong.

*Fritz:*   Again.

*Louise:*   When I go at it, I can squish you, and it's just my *allowing* you to be, just the fact that I let you *exist,* is the only reason that you aren't.

*Fritz:* Chalk?

*Louise:* (As chalk, peering out from under a hand, hunched foreward) You wouldn't do that. You wouldn't do that. You haven't got the right to do that.

*Fritz:* Now write the script yourself. Change roles whenever you feel like it.

*Louise:* (As book) So you thing you can write all over me, huh? What makes you think that? If I want to, I could kill you. Just you open your mouth one more time, and I'll squash you. 'Cause besides putting you between my pages and slowly squishing you like that (she rolls over), I can just get up and drop myself all over you (she does so.) (As chalk) Ha ha haha haha haha, you may have squished me, but I'm still here. You can't get rid of me, I'm still here. Now I'm dust, and I can cover you if I want to, cover you all up with my dust. (Pause) But I don't know what that would do. I think I'd rather just leave you. Leave you to fret and fume. (Pause. She pulls at her lip with her left hand.)

*Fritz:* What is your left hand doing now?

*Louise:* Twisting my lip.

*Fritz:* Ya? (She continues to play with her lip, looking thoughtful.) I would like you now to be the professor again. Tell the class about your conflict—what the right hand does and what the left hand does.

*Louise:* (Standing up) I'd better turn around and face the class.

*Fritz:* Professor, what do you see when you face the class? Do you see the class?

*Louise:* No.

*Fritz:* Say this to the class.

*Louise:* (As professor; harsh voice) Class, I look at you and I can't even see you. You all sort of melt together into one big frightening shape.

*Fritz:* Now change position. Be the class. Talk back to the professor.

*Louise:* (As class, standing on one leg, arms akimbo, sarcastic) Who in the hell do you think we are, anyway? You're the one who has the grades to give, you're the one who can let us pass or not let us pass. It's not up to us to do anything about you; we don't *like* you.

*Fritz:*   Say this again.

*Louise:*   We don't like you.

*Fritz:*   Tell him what you don't like about him.

*Louise:*   (Aggressive) We don't like the goddamn fact that you don't even look at us, that you don't even care what the hell is going on. You'd just as soon be satisfied with your work. That's full of a lot of crap, and I think you know it.

*Fritz:*   Be the professor again.

*Louise:*   (As professor, feet close together, belligerent, whining.) I've told you how I felt, I told you that I can't even see you, and you come back and are ready to stomp all over me, ready to squish me. How do you think that makes *me* feel. You're so concerned about how . . . how *you* feel, but how do you think that makes *me* feel?

*Fritz:*   Change roles again.

*Louise:*   (As class) So goddamn what? What are we supposed to do, sit up here and try to make you feel good? Is that all right? All I want in life? Is that what you think?

*Fritz:*   Say this to Mary. (Laughter) Do you still need approval? (More laughing)

*Louise:*   (To Mary) Mary, what do you think we're here for, to make you feel good? What the goddamn hell is this, anyway? (Laughter) You're so full of shit, I love you.

*Fritz:*   What's going on ow?

*Louise:*   I feel like turning around, sitting down, backing away.

*Fritz:*   Back away. Now close your eyes and go away, leave this room. Leave this room just in fantasy. Where would you go?

*Louise:*   (Eyes closed) I'd go for a walk down to the path to the water, down by the beach.

*Fritz:*   Ya. What do you experience there?

*Louise:*   (Quietly, eyes closed, still standing) I like to walk in the sand and feel the cold wet sand between my feet (she wriggles toes) and it goes up between my toes and down between my toes, and it feels good. It feels solid. (She makes a few slow, tentative steps.) Then I'll sit down for a minute, just look at the water. (She sits crosslegged, arms on knees.) It doesn't last for very long.

*Fritz:*   Come back to us now. How do you experience being here?

*Louise:*   (Eyes open, sitting) Kind of shaky, but basically good.

*Fritz:*   Can you dance the shakiness now?

(She constructs a dance, bringing her hands to her hair, stretching, and brings her hands forward, curled inward and reaching; a few small steps, and she makes contact with somebody's foot and stumbles. Her shoulders are tight, contracted; then she opens and stretches over in a tentlike movement, very tense, and then releases, arms hanging loose at sides, taking small, quiet steps, quiet and easy.)

*Fritz:*   Now do you see us? How are your eyes, still not clear?

*Louise:*   (Quiet, intense) Yeah, I think I see people. You are people. I think I see you.

*Fritz:*   All right. Be the professor again. Face the classroom again.

*Louise:*   (As professor; quiet, relaxed, intent) Class, I can see a little of what's going on. I see . . . many eyes around. I see . . . you have many eyes, that you wear glasses, some of you. Some of you don't. You have blue eyes and brown eyes . . . some glasses flashing . . .

*Fritz:*   You still see essentially eyes. You don't have eyes yet, your eyes are still on the outside. So play the different eyes looking at you. See the way you can see the professor now. Look at him again. Be the eyes of the class.

*Louise:*   (As eyes; sits down crosslegged, arms on knees.) There are several different eyes in the class. They are brown eyes with glasses on. They're coming towards me.

*Fritz:*   The eyes, you are not yet the eyes. The eyes are still outside. Could you be the brown eyes? (Pause) As brown eyes, what are you doing with the professor?

*Louise:*   Holding the professor.

*Fritz:*   Say this to him.

*Louise:*   Professor, we want to hold you. (Pause) For some reason, I'm at knee level and upper legs. . .

*Fritz:*   Now be some of the other eyes. Be the blue eyes. How do you encounter the professor?

*Louise:* Blue eyes. As blue eyes, I see the professor, but I see more than professor.

*Fritz:* Say this to him.

*Louise:* Professor, I see you, but in you I see more than you. Seeing you helps me to—me to see into myself—my own hurts. I like you, but now I'm thinking more of me. I must go away just a bit for now. I'm in my own world now. (She makes a gesture of pushing away, concentrates inward.)

*Fritz:* (Pause) What happened?

*Louise:* What happened?

*Fritz:* Yah. Where are you now? . . . Where are you now?

*Louise:* Not as here as I was.

*Fritz:* You left us again. Now withdraw again. Let us know where you are going.

*Louise:* (She dances again, sitting. She opens her arms, eyes closed, feeling and groping outward, then brings her arms together around her and looks out from under them. She crouches together and looks down intently and then curls inward into a fetal crouch. Pause. She stands up.) I'm going down into the earth.

*Fritz:* Ya. What do you find there? What do you discover there?

*Louise:* It's rich and brown . . . and the little pebbles . . . and there is a snail. It's a brown snail with a small shell and it's . . . small.

*Fritz:* Now be the brown snail. What kind of existence do you lead, brown snail?

*Louise:* (She goes back into a crouching, snail-like position, moving as a snail as she talks, knees and elbows on the floor.) I live in my shell, but when I want to, I can put part of me out of my shell (she moves foreward, crouched) and I can move that away.

*Fritz:* Come back and say the sentence to us.

*Louise:* (In snail position) I live in my shell. Sometimes I can come out of it a little ways, and that's how I can move . . . and I bring my shell up (mimes) and then I come out of it again, a little ways, then I stretch and I put my feelers out and I look around, and I pull up again. But I like being a snail. I like being . . . In fact, even my shell is kind of pretty sometimes (feels along shell spiral) if you really look at the design of my shell, it has spirals on it, lots of very small lines going crisscross around the spirals . . . very intricate.

*Fritz:*  Snail, I take your house away now. I leave you naked. See what you experience now, without the shell.

*Louise:*  (Contracting into a shell) Well, I pull up into myself without the shell to protect me.

*Fritz:*  Say this again.

*Louise:*  There is nothing to protect me, when I pull into myself.

*Fritz:*  What are you afraid of? What do you need protection from?

*Louise:*  People with big feet and heavy shoes, who will walk on me. (She mimes a naked snail, contracting away.)

*Fritz:*  Now be that person; walk on the snail with big feet and heavy shoes.

*Louise:*  (Standing, walking with big feet, deliberately placing her feet) Kind of an unconscious act. I'm not really conscious of stepping on the snail.

*Fritz:*  Step on us. We're all snails now.

*Louise:*  Gosh. (She walks around circle, slowly and deliberately placing her feet, walking over the feet of people in the circle; she walks on Mary's feet and there is laughter.)

*Fritz:*  How do you feel when you do that?

*Louise:*  A combination of nonchalant and guilty. (Still walking.) I've been on the other side. There's a kind of freedom and joy to walk where I want to. If there's a snail in the way, well . . . it's in the way.

*Fritz:*  Say this to the snails—to us: "If you're in my way . . ."

*Louise:*  Well, snails, (loud) if you happen to be in my way when I'm just walking along, well, that's death. If you don't think I'm heavy, try it out!

*Fritz:*  Say this to Mary.

*Louise:*  (To Mary) If you're in my way, babes, you go too, and that's just the way it is. Fritz (walks on him), you too.

*Fritz:*  How are your eyes now? What do you see?

*Louise:*  They're good.

*Fritz:*  Do you see us?

*Louise:*   Yes.

*Fritz:*   Clearly?

*Louise:*   I think so there are arms too . . . besides eyes there are arms. (She sits down and wraps her arms about her, leans back smiling and smoking a cigarette.)

*Fritz:*   All right. That is as far as I want to go.

## Martha*

*Fritz:*   I would call the case of Martha the case of a delayed reaction. In most cases, I am capable of getting into the center of a person and solving some relevant situation in—definitely within an hour. Now the case of Martha showed some difficulties in this respect. I worked with her the day before for a short time, and it clearly showed up that her difficulty with the previous therapy was that her curtain was not discovered. When she got in difficulties, she drew a mental curtain between herself and the therapist so no communication was possible. She did not *play* stupid, she actually became blank and incapable of communicating. This curtain will, in a different form, appear in this film too.

If I have a dream to work with, then the therapy is very much simplified. My dream technique consists of using all kinds of available material that is invested in the dream. I let the people play the different parts and, if they are capable of really entering the spirit of that part, they are assimilating their disowned material. As you see, Martha is so much out of touch, has got so rigid and dead, that she has great difficulties in really entering the spirit of the different roles. She tries; she is of good will, but she can't quite make it. But in spite of this, something will happen.

After we finished our session, then a delayed reaction came and she had a breakthrough to emotionalism. Before, there is hardly any affect and feeling visible. The language is rigid, her ability to go along with the therapist is rather handicapped. There are parts of the film that will appear very boring to you because nothing happens on the surface. But still, bit by bit, something has been assimilated and the idea is to show that in spite of the unsatisfactory outcome,

*Media—Psych Corporation

still something very important did happen.

(Martha is a young woman of about twenty-five. She is attractive in appearance, but her manner is flat, she speaks in a monotone, her posture is hunched and listless. She is sitting in the chair next to Dr. Perls (the hot seat) and facing her is an empty chair.)

*Martha:* Uh—I've had variations of this dream. I—ah—am walking and there's a—a church, and it's a midwestern brick church, just a little long building, small but long. And over on the side there's a kitchen. And the kitchen to the church is all open on one side. And I walk into the room and there is a Negro woman—she's an older woman—and her name is Druggers or something like that. And I seem to say something to her. And then I see this other woman walking in.

*Fritz:* Who is this other woman?

*Martha:* I don't know who she is. A middle-aged woman. She walks in, and I know that something is really going to happen. I have a feeling this woman is going to kill this woman. And so I get—upset, and—um—I walk through this corridor into the church. And I go up to this man and he is the vice-principal of the school I taught at. And I say, Ron, there's going to be a murder in this room—in a room—in the kitchen. This woman's going to kill this woman. And he just looks at me, and says it's all taken care of. And then I look up at the front of the church and I see four men sitting there. One man just turns his head a little bit to the side, and it's my father. So I go back to the kitchen and—um—there are a lot of young boys, and they're on the phone and they're talking to the police. And the body is out on the lawn, all covered over with just a—a—canvas or something. And they said: "Just leave the body out there." And then I walk out and I have to go up a hill and I have to walk through all this brains and junk—garbage and all that.

*Fritz:* Yah. Well, let's first play a few roles until we do the whole thing. I don't know whether we have time. Now I—Play the church: "I am a midwestern church—"

*Martha:* Uh—I'm a church made of brick.

*Fritz:* I'm made out of brick.

*Martha:* And I have—ah—just a linoleum floor, there's

no carpet. And I—ah—have hard benches.

*Fritz:*   And what's your purpose, church?

*Martha:*   (She has a baffled look and speaks with hesitation, as though through a fog.) Uh—

*Fritz:*   Where are you?

*Martha:*   My life—

*Fritz:*   Yah, yah.

*Martha:*   My whole life—

*Fritz:*   You are blocking something. When you told the dream you said and, and, and; no pauses. Now, suddenly, when I ask you something, you have a curtain come down again. What do you experience now?

*Martha:*   I'm—kind of scared about something. I have—memories—of the church and what the church means—I think the church—where I was when I was little—But it's not that church, it's not that one—

*Fritz:*   You're not the same church as when you were little?

*Martha:*   I'm not—No, the memory I just had is not the same church as the church when I was little.

*Fritz:*   All right. Now play this Negro woman.

*Martha:*   She is—

*Fritz:*   I am—

*Martha:*   I am—

*Fritz:*   You see—ah—let me explain something to you. We are very impoverished in our potential. We have disowned a lot of what we could be. We have alienated lots of our potential, and to take it back we have to re-identify it. And we do it in this dream work by becoming—by really playing—being this part that we have alienated. Now, I want you really to be that Negro woman. You don't understand yet? Which part of you is the Negro woman? But if you really play it out, you'll understand it.

*Martha:*   (Strained voice, as through an obstacle) I am—tall and—calm and—kindly—and working in the kitchen. Feel very competent—very warm—

*Fritz:*   Now play this other woman—middle-aged woman.

*Martha:*   I'm insane—and very distraught—and just walking and very—uh—with full intent—of killing—and I even have a knife—

*Fritz:*   You want to kill that Negro woman?

*Martha:*   Ya, I'm just going to come right in around that table and kill her.

*Fritz:*   How would you kill her.

*Martha:*   —just hack—just give a strong hack.

*Fritz:*   What's your objection to her?

*Martha:*   I don't know.

*Fritz:*   What's your objection to her?

*Martha:*   (Long pause)—it's like she was waiting for me—

*Fritz:*   Have an encounter with her: "I came here to kill you—"

*Martha*   It seems senseless—like it's not without—with any thought—but just to walk over there and just—hit her.

*Fritz:*   Now be the dead woman, the dead Negro woman. Play her.

*Martha:*   But in the dream, the woman who was killed wasn't the Negro. (Pause) She is the white woman, and she's just laying out there in the grass.

*Fritz:*   Play her.

*Martha:*   I'm just—My body has been thrown out on the grass because they said—just leave it there—Just thrown out and—I'm on my back—and there's a canvas over—over what's left. (Pause.)

*Fritz:*   Now be the canvas: "I am the canvas—"

*Martha:*   I am a canvas—and rough—and I cover up what's left—so other people don't have to see it—

*Fritz:*   Now play the people who want to see it —underneath the canvas.

*Martha:*   Nobody wants to see it—they're just—um —standing around—one's talking on the phone, the Negro woman isn't there any more. They're just a lot of these —boys—standing around—

*Fritz:*   Play the boys now.

*Martha:*   I'm milling around—

*Fritz:*   We are, we are—Come, play it, play it, play it.

*Martha:*   They're just—we're just standing around.

*Fritz:*   Yah.

*Martha:*   —waiting for the police to come and—and

take care of the mess.

*Fritz:*   Play the police.

*Martha:*   —Just have a bag—I have a bag, and we'll just put the mess in here—and take it off, cart it away—

*Fritz:*   Now be the dead woman again. You're being carried away.

*Martha:*   —I'm—being wrapped up so nobody has to see it—and the—just carried away—

*Fritz:*   What are they doing to—with you?

*Martha:*   It's their job to pick me up and—

*Fritz:*   And do what with you?

*Martha:*   Throw the remains away some place.

*Fritz:*   Where to? Give me the place that they are throwing you.

*Martha:*   —Morgue—

*Fritz:*   Yah.

*Martha:*   —and—

*Fritz:*   Martha, when did you die?

*Martha:*   (Flat voice, with strain) I don't remember—I don't even remember—I just don't even remember ever being alive, not even as a child. I can't even remember—I don't remember. Sometimes I just feel like I just—just screamed and—died.

*Fritz:*   Go back and be the church again.

*Martha:*   —I'm silent—and old— (Pause.)

*Fritz:*   What do you experience now?

*Martha:*   I feel just—have just a lot of memories of church—

*Fritz:*   Now I want you to interrupt this for a moment and come back to us here. Come back to reality from your nightmare, from your death. Look around. What do you see? How do you experience the world at this moment.

*Martha:*   I think pretty warm.

*Fritz:*   What do you experience?

*Martha:*   People are—um—caring—

*Fritz:*   Yah?

*Martha:*   —I feel like I'm cared for—

*Fritz:*   What about yourself? The boys don't care, apparently.

*Fritz:*   What about your caring? Look around. Could

you care for anybody here?

*Martha:*   Yeah

*Fritz:*   Can you express it?

*Martha:*   Well, I know there are two people here especially that I care very, very, very, very much for.

*Fritz:*   Don't gossip about it. Express it. Say that to them. Go.

*Martha:*   (Strained little laugh) I don't even know how to tell somebody—how to return (very strained, hard voice)—how I can return—how nice you are to me—and I—wish I could somehow—help you not to be so damned afraid—

*Fritz:*   Now listen to your voice. You're not talking to them.

*Martha:*   No, I'm—I can't—

*Fritz:*   You are producing literature, not communication. Try once more. Go over and say this to her.

*Martha:*   —I don't know how.

*Fritz:*   Now get up and—You're sitting again at cross-purposes. As I showed you before—the right hand goes to the left and the left hand goes to the right. How can you live like that? How can you do that? Now go like this to her. (He opens his arms wide.)

*Martha:*   (She imitates Fritz's open gesture and speaks with a noticeably surer voice.) Yeah, I guess I wish I could tell you when you make me mad and when you make me angry and then I wish I could tell you when I feel that I really care for you, how you feel and how you are.

*Fritz:*   Still literature.

*Martha:*   Damn.

*Fritz:*   Damn, yah. Just damn it. Try again. Start with Marykay.

*Martha:*   All right. Right now—why I get upset—because I feel you ask me to like you—and then you won't let me—like you—or to tell you or to show you or—

*Fritz:*   Call her a few names. Tell her what she is: "Meany—"

*Martha:*   —I—

*Fritz:*   Can you feel your emotional constipation?

*Martha:*   Yeah, damn, I sure can.

*Fritz:* Now go over to her, now. Go over to her. Close your eyes and just touch her with your fingertips. (Martha goes over to stand in front of Marykay, a young woman on the other side of the group, and puts her hands on Marykay's shoulders. Marykay reaches up to respond.) No. No, don't respond, please. Just let her get in touch with you. (To Martha) What do your hands feel?

*Martha:* —She's warm—

*Fritz:* Say: "You are warm." Always speak in the second person.

*Martha:* You are warm.

*Fritz:* Let your fingers tell us what they feel. Go on. Go on exploring her.

*Martha:* You're soft—and you're afraid—(Sigh)—

*Fritz:* So what do you experience now?

*Martha:* —I'm afraid—

*Fritz:* So come back. Come back. (Martha goes and sits in her chair next to Fritz again.) Now look again around. What do you feel now?

*Martha:* I feel like the curtain is down.

*Fritz:* The curtain is down again. You're dead again. Okay. Where shall we bury the corpse. (Fritz takes Martha's hand.) You are not completely dead. Your hands are lukewarm, they are not really icy. You still have possibilities for a ressurection. You have to work on it.

*(Change of scene to studio)*

*Fritz:* I guess you noticed at least two things in this film. One is that this curtain came back as the canvas and that behind this curtain actually was death, this debris, the lost life. The other interesting thing is after I asked her, "When did you die," that then we found the first trace of emotionalism. She started to grieve over her own death. Then, after we had finished the session, I walked out. Afterwards I looked back and then I saw that actually the grief had taken over and that she cried profusely and was comforted by her friends. We are going to see this last scene right now.

(Change of scene back to the group. Martha is in the middle of a group of people, crying bitterly and being comforted.)

## A Session With College Students*

This is a transcript of a Gestalt Therapy session. About fifteen young men and women are sitting in a circle. They are college students. Dr. Perls is in the circle, with an empty chair next to him. This is the "hot seat"—any one of the group who wants to work with Dr. Perls may get up and sit in the hot seat. Opposite the hot seat there is another empty chair. The session is being filmed, and there are cameras and microphones about. As a person works, he or she takes the hot seat and may occasionally change seats to the other empty chair.

*Fritz:* Now, this is the hot seat. You all know this by now. And this is the empty chair. That's the part that you have to deal with, whether this is part of yourself or part of somebody you carry with you, somebody with whom you haven't got the situation finished. Right now we are in a studio, and we just talked about the stage fright. Gestalt therapy is exclusively interested in the *now* and our aim is to learn to cope with whatever happens, and right now what happens is a certain amount of stage fright. If you feel uncomfortable you are not in honest communication. So let's sample a bit. Will you take the hot seat? (A young woman takes the hot seat.) And tell me how you experience your stage fright.

*Barbara:* —Uh—my hands are very cold and wet. Very wet. And I have this little paper. (Twists piece of paper. Giggles.)

*Fritz:* Can you do this to me?

*Barbara:* Tearing you?

*Fritz:* Yeah.

*Barbara:* Yes.

*Fritz:* Come. Tear me apart.

*Barbara:* (Twisting paper) I'm scared to death. I'm scared of you.

* Media-Psych Corporation

*Fritz:* Put me in that chair (indicates empty chair).

*Barbara:* And talk to you?

*Fritz:* Yes.

*Barbara:* I think—I guess I'm afraid because I think *I'll do something to myself;* because I know you aren't going to do anything to me. But I really am afraid of you.

*Fritz:* Okay, now switch over to the camera. Say this to the camera.

*Barbara:* (Looking at the camera) I really am afraid of you.

*Fritz:* Now, play the camera. Sit down here and play the camera. What would the camera answer? If you had some feeling as the camera, what would you say? Talk to that girl who was so frightened.

*Barbara:* (Changes seats and speaks as the camera) I see you sitting there; I see you nervous; I see you unsure—I see you as *okay.* (She gives a relieved sigh.)

*Fritz:* Now be yourself again. What would you say? Go on with the dialogue.

*Barbara:* I feel better. I'm not so—ah—concerned right now. I feel more at ease.

*Fritz:* Yeah. You see, this always happens. If you assimilate some of the projection and you realize that you are dealing actually with a fantasy, something you invent, *and if you take back what you have given up—whatever energy or experience you have disowned,* given to the world,—then it becomes your own. Then you grow, you integrate this foreign material. All right, let's—Will you try this? Take the hot seat. (A second young woman takes the hot seat.)

*Ann:* My palms are very cold and wet, and I'm going inside very fast. Right there. But otherwise I feel supernaturally calm.

*Fritz:* Ah. *Supernaturally* calm.

*Ann:* Yes.

*Fritz:* So it might be that your calmness is phoney.

*Ann:* Yeah. Yeah.

*Fritz:* All right, now close your eyes. Withdraw into your body. What do you feel physically?

*Ann:* Hammer, hammer, hammer, hammer.

*Fritz:* Can you exaggerate this hammer, hammer?

Make noises.

*Ann:*　Ach. Ach. Hach. Hanch.

*Fritz:*　Louder.

*Anna:*　(Makes loud, harsh breathing noises.) That sure feels better. (General laughter.)

*Fritz:*　That's right.

(Ann returns to her seat, and another young woman takes the hot seat.)

*Dorothy:*　I'm still playing with a paper.

*Fritz:*　Talk to the paper.

*Dorothy:*　Paper, I'm still winding you up. Won't let you go. *And my hands* are still sweaty and they're shaking a little bit. And—uh—I'm getting a little hot. (Victimized by her hand!)

*Fritz:*　Do you hear your voice?

*Dorothy:*　Yeah. I'm getting scared.

*Fritz:*　*Of what? (Not why.)*

*Dorothy:*　Of all those people out there watching me.

*Fritz:*　Tell this to them.

*Dorothy:*　I'm scared of all you people out there watching me.

*Fritz:*　Now change position. You're one of the people out there watching you. Say: I'm seeing you—"

*Dorothy:*　I'm seeing you, and you *should* be scared. Especially if my parents are watching or something like that, and I say something—It may hurt you.

*Fritz:*　Okay, change seats again. Talk back.

*Dorothy:*　(Changes seats) I've got a lot of hostility against the whole crowd and my parents.

*Fritz:*　Express your hostility. Express it on this piece of paper.

*Dorothy:*　I'd like to wind you up.

*Fritz:*　Tell this to us.

*Dorothy:*　I'd like to wind you all up.

*Fritz:*　Now, in this, I notice you have disowned your own eyes. Instead of having eyes, the eyes are in the outside world and they are looking at you.

*Dorothy:*　Yeah. Right.

*Fritz:*　Now, could you try to discover your own eyes, and tell us what you see? Use your eyes now. What do you see?

*Dorothy:* I see that I'm scared—

*Fritz:* That's not what you see. That's what you imagine.

*Dorothy:* All I see, then are cameras—and shapes—

*Fritz:* Yeah.

*Dorothy:* And darkness.

*Fritz:* Do you see me?

*Dorothy:* —and just people sitting there. (Tone changes.)

*Fritz:* Ah! You're waking up. Yeah. This is what I call the mini-satori. In contrast to the great satori—the great waking up. This is a little waking up. Suddenly, one wakes out of a trance, like—You are being persecuted by the eyes of the world.

*Dorothy:* Yes.

(Dorothy sits in her own seat, and another young woman takes the hot seat.)

*Judy:* I have very cold, sweaty hands, and my feet——And my toes are separated from my body—I can't feel them at all.

*Fritz:* Talk to them.

*Judy:* Toes, why are you so cold—and dirty? I feel the sandals confining. I want to crack my toes. I feel confined by the sandals.

*Fritz:* Now let your toes talk to the sandals: "I feel confined by you—"

*Judy:* Let me go, sandals. I want to move.

*Fritz:* Again.

*Judy:* Let me go.

*Fritz:* Scream it.

*Judy:* LET ME GO!

*Fritz:* Again.

*Judy:* LET ME GO, SANDALS! (She returns to her seat.)

*Fritz:* Now, the way to cope with dreams in Gestalt therapy is this: We consider dreams as an existential message, not a residual of unfinished situations or traumatic things or wish-fulfillment. And we have to find out what is the message we get from our dreams. There is something else in the dream that has to be understood. A dream is a fragmentation of our personality. Now, by fragmentation, I mean this: If I have three peices of wood, and I put them together into a triangle, then this triangel forms a Gestalt, a coherent one. Now, if they are again taken apart, they are fragmented—they are all over. So. Much of our personality is fragmented. It's there, but it's not available because the different parts are separated from each other. Now, Gestalt therapy is not an analytical, but an integrative method. And the main thing is—if we work with dreams—not to interpret, not to play interpretation and intellectual games. I believe any interpretation is a therapeutic mistake. And interpretation is an interference of the therapist's opinion, on the patient. So the patient has to do all the dirty work by himself. And the steps we do are—

(Ann has again taken the hot seat, and Fritz speaks to her) We *first* ask: Will you tell us the dream.)

*Ann:* Yeah. I was in a long, dark, cold place—possibly a cement bunker or sewer, underground, with my children. None of us were wearing clothes, and we had some scuba diving equipment—kind of hoses—and I knew I had to get out and I knew I had to get them out. And I got very angry at them, and started hitting them and yelling at them, but it didn't make—I never could contact their flesh. I hit them very, very hard.

*Fritz:* Uhuh. Now we know already one of the existential messages. You avoid getting in touch, and hitting the children. You see that?

*Ann:* In my life, I hit them a lot.

*Fritz:* And in the dream—

*Ann:* I don't. I don't feel very good about hitting them when I do.

*Fritz:* Now, this is the first step. The second step is, I make you now a stage director. Will you set the stage for the dream? And talk in the present tense. Build up the stage in fantasy: "I am here with my children. There's the sewage."

*Ann:* Okay. (Stands up and moves around as she describes setting.) I'm in a cold, dark place. The walls are cold on either side of me. And my kids, I think, are ahead of me. But they aren't going fast enough. And I say, *"Come on, let's go!* And I keep hitting them and hitting them and hitting them and hitting them. (She acts this out as she says it.) And they just kind of stand there. I just never get through to them. It's like hitting a vacuum.

*Fritz:* Now play the child. And talk to your mother.

*Ann:* I'm not going to move. And you certainly are working up a storm. And I'm just not going to move. And you can knock yourself out. And I'm not going to do a damn thing. I'm going to go exactly the way I want to go. (To Fritz) It stopped there. I forgot it there.

*Fritz:* Yes. All right. Now, let's have a real encounter with your child. Now be the child again. It's a he or she—?

*Ann:* Both.

*Fritz:* Both. Okay. They are defying you.

*Ann:* Shall I take that seat? (Indicates the other chair.)

*Fritz:* Yah.

*Ann:* (Changes seats; speaking as children.) You can't catch me. You can't hurt me. You sure are making a fool of yourself, yelling and hitting, and I'm going to go at my own pace. You can't rush me.

*Fritz:* What would you answer?

*Ann:* (Speaking as mother) You've got to get out of here! I know what's good for you, and I have to get you out of here. And that's the most important thing. Listen to me. And look at me.

*Fritz:* (Gesturing toward other chair) There again.

*Ann:* (Switches chair; speaking as child) Unless you really hit me, you won't get anything. You can just stir up as much mud as you want. But you're not going to get to me until I'm just ready for it.

*Frtiz:* Now, can you talk to me like your children, as yourself?

*Ann:* (Childish voice) I don't want to do it! Leave me alone! Go away and stop bothering me! Anghhh——

*Fritz:* Now be your own age, and talk in the same spirit. But express yourself as you are to me.

*Ann:* (Quiet voice) Just leave me alone. You can't touch me. You can't do a thing to me. You can strike out, you can look away, you can be bored. But it doesn't make any difference.

*Fritz:* What kind of a person are you playing now?

*Ann:* It's a mixture. It's very haughty—

*Fritz:* Yah.

*Ann:* —and it's a little tiny bit seductive. (She gives a sign). The dream was so powerful when it was happening. It had the strongest physical response I've ever had from a dream. An unpleasant one. And I don't know why it isn't even stronger—why I'm not going into orbit with it. You know. Maybe it's such a stalemate.

*Fritz:* All right. Do you feel anything of this still now?

*Ann:* I can summon it up. I'll tell you why I thought the dream was so important to me after I had it. Because when I get very angry, I turn off that anger, or I used to turn it in. In. Just like that (speaks in a strained voice). And I'm not really going to hurt myself, but I tried as hard as I could. Sometimes I even pinch myself *(she pinches herself)*. But I was never going to—

*Fritz:* Do this to me. Now, I notice when you do this, you hold your breath.

*Ann:Yeah. Oh, it's real* holding breath.

*Fritz:* Yah. Now do it again, and breathe at the same time. (She pinches his hand, breathing deeply.) Go on breathing, and make noises.

*Ann:* (Noisy exhaling and inhaling.)

*Fritz:* How do you feel now?

*Ann:* A lot more power.

*Fritz:* You see, now you have re-owned some power from the dream. In the dream, you were impotent.

*Ann:* Yeah.

*Fritz:* Now we have taken some of the power of the children away from them and given it back to you.

*Ann:* Yeah. I think I lash out at them and then I take it back immediately into myself.

*Fritz:* Yah, yah.

*Ann:* Ohhh—They'll get it tomorrow! (Alive.) (Fritz laughs) Thank you. (She goes back to her own seat.)

*Fritz:* So even if you don't consider the whole dream —if you do it on your own— if you dream and you just play the different parts and understand—at least *try* to confront each other, have a lot of internal encounters—until again you reassimilate more and more of your disowned material—in this case your power and all that you did to yourself by doing it to me—you become more real. Because this is the essence of Gestalt therapy. We want to change paper people into real people. This is why we discard all opinion playing and interpretation and so on. So. Who wants to work on a dream next? (Speaks to Barbara) You?

*Barbara:*   I have a dream.

*Fritz:*   Ya. (Barbara takes hot seat) In order to make a shortcut, let's do something on the surface phony. Tell me your dream and intersperse each sentence with "this is my existence." In order to understand this is not just a scene, it is the basic structure of your existence.

*Barbara:*   I should speak in the now for this dream, I think. I am on top of a tall tower. This is my existence.

*Fritz:*   I have to interrupt you, because there's something, some expression, going on. Don't interrupt it, please. Tell me what you are doing with your hands.

*Barbara:*   (Faintly) I don't know.

*Fritz:*   Let your right hand talk to your left hand.

*Barbara:*   I am rubbing you. I feel—It feels good to press hard, to squeeze those fingers. I—I like to squeeze you.

*Fritz:*   Say this again.

*Barbara:*   *I like to squeeze you.*

*Fritz:*   Now, what does your left hand answer?

*Barbara:*   I am passive. I like that. I—I feel good.

*Fritz:*   Now, we don't know yet to what degree we find here a right-left split. The right hand—the right side —usually expresses the male, aggressive, motoric, practical side. So. All right, let's go back to the dream.

*Barbara:*   Is that the same if you're right-handed or left-handed?

*Fritz:*   Yes.

*Barbara:*   I'm on top of a tower and the tower is going around. It's a tall tower. I am thrown off the edge and I am clinging over the side, and this is my existence. And I'm hanging onto the railing and I'm falling—

*Fritz:*   You really experience this?

*Barbara:*   Yes. And I'm clinging and holding on as hard as I can and I'm calling for help.

*Fritz:*   How?

*Barbara:* I'm calling: Help! Help me! And I'm calling my husband, who is sitting inside, and he doesn't hear me. And—uh—my children are there someplace, also.

*Fritz:* Now put your husband in that chair and call to him for help.

*Barbara:* Bob! Bob! Bob! Come and help me, Bob! I'm falling. Come and help me. Please come and help me!

*Fritz:* Do you hear your voice? Can you hear your voice? Say it again, and see if your voice expresses what you feel.

*Barbara:* Bob! Come and help me, Bob. Come and help me. I need your help, Bob. I need you.

*Fritz:* Say this again.

*Barbara:* I need you.

*Fritz:* Again.

*Barbara:* (Crying a little) I need you.

*Fritz:* Again.

*Barbara:* I need you.

*Fritz:* What does he answer?

*Barbara:* (Changes seats; speaking as Bob) I don't mean not to hear you. I just didn't hear you. I just didn't notice. (Crying) I just didn't notice. I want to help you.

*Fritz:* Take your seat again. What would you say to him?

*Barbara:* (Changing seats) I'm mad because you don't hear me. It seems like you don't care. (Changes seats again; speaking as Bob) I do care, Bobby.

*Fritz:* Say this again.

*Barbara:* I do care, Bobby.

*Fritz:* Again.

*Barbara:* I do care, Bobby.

*Fritz:* Change again.

*Barbara:* (Crying) I want to embrace him.

*Fritz:* Do this.

*Barbara:* He's not here. (She embraces an imaginery Bob.)

*Fritz:* Did he get the message?

*Barbara:* (Sniffling) I don't—I don't know.

*Fritz:* But you understand; there's something wrong with your communication.

*Barbara:* Yes.

*Fritz:* (Interpretation)—and you play the blaming game. He is to be blamed. It could be that you don't know how to touch him—how to communicate with him. Well, there is so much more in the dream. Your desperate clinging and so on. But I think we are—want to—finish up. At least you got a little bit from this dream, right? (Barbara nods.) I think we learned something very important in the last session: this is involvement. We started out being involved with the situation here and everyone had stage fright. And now that some other Gestalt emerges, like the dream work, you got so involved in your own happening that then the background recedes. You become real in a different way. Now, one could take one dream and take up every little item. Not just the different people, but the different things. And this would be enough to achieve complete integration. But what usually happens is that after a dream is worked through and some of the fragmented pieces integrated, we get another dream that shows more what's going on and already simplifies. You see, expecially when you have these nightmares, which are the real self-frustration dreams, and you stop frustrating yourself, you stop interfering with yourself, then you start to blossom out and be in touch with the world and so on. So let's have another try at dreams. (Speaks to Judy) Will you come? Now, again, go back into the dream. As long as you dream, the dream seems to be absolutely real. The most absurd dream appears to be real and this is absolutely justified—because what you dream *is* real. It's a different language. (Judy sits in the hot seat) So. What is your dream?

*Judy:* I was in a department store, like Macy's.

*Fritz:* Talk in the present tense. Enter the dream.

*Judy:* I am in a department store. But it doesn't have any limit to the floors. It goes on and on and on. You can go up the escalator. My mother was waiting outside, in the cold, and she was hunched shouldered. In a black coat. And I went in to go shopping. And—

*Fritz:* You see that you immediately killed the aliveness of the dream and—ah—Well, I don't yet expect from you a real cooperation. And also, the dream confirms this. But at least try to stay in the present tense.

*Judy:*   I am in a department store.

*Fritz:*   Your mother is waiting outside.

*Judy:*   My mother is waiting outside. She's in a black coat.

*Fritz:*   What are you doing with your left hand?

*Judy:*   I'm chopping my leg.

*Fritz:*   You're chopping your leg. Go on chopping your leg. Whom else do you want to chop?

*Judy:*   My mother. (Gives a little laugh.)

*Fritz:*   (Interpretation but *good*) Now chop her. And at the same time, it indicates that your mother is your leg. All right now, let's start with this little fragment of the dream. If you were this department store, what kind of an existence would you lead? You are now this department store.

*Judy:*   I am the department store?

*Fritz:*   Yah.

*Judy:*   I'd be big, and—

*Fritz:*   I *am* big, and—

*Judy:*   I have many things inside my stomach. I hold everything. Everything in the world. it's all here. Anything you want, you can find inside me. There are books and records and furniture and I have clothes—

*Fritz:*   Now, can you listen to your voice? Can you play your voice?

*Judy:*   Like an instrument? (Sings: La-a-a-a-a-a.)

*Fritz:*   This is not how I hear your voice. I hear your voice: (he grunts) un-uh-un-uh-uh—

*Judy:*   I can't hear it.

*Fritz:*   That's right. You don't hear your own voice. All right now. Be your mother.

*Judy:*   (Whining voice, as mother) Judy—Judy—Where are you? What are you doing? Why don't you call me?

*Fritz:*   Talk back.

*Judy:*   Because I'm not you. I'm not you! You don't know—You don't *have* to know everything that's happening in my life.

*Fritz:*   Change seats.

*Judy:*   (Changes seats; as mother) But—I'm all alone now—I don't have anybody any more.

154

*Fritz:* So, go on writing this script between you and your mother.

*Judy:* (As self) Uh—*I have to be myself.* I want to tell you. 'Cause you never listen. But—I have to live my own life. I'm not you.

*Fritz:* Does she hear you? Does she hear You?

*Judy:* (As mother) What? I don't think you're me. I—I don't expect you to be like me. I have my own life. You know that. (Changes seats; as self) But—But you're there. You don't go away.

*Fritz:* Let's do something phony. Let your mother go into the department store. Say what you would experience there. Play your mother in the department store.

*Judy:* Well—(As mother) Judy, look, here's a nice dress. Don't you think this would look good on you? It shouldn't make you look older. Let's see what size it is. Oh, it's a nine. Do you think a nine will fit?

*Fritz:* Okay. Now you are allowed to talk back to her, or talk with her. What she says—wouldn't this fit and so on.

*Judy:* (As self) But I don't like that. I don't like the color. (As mother) But—what color do you want? (As self) I want red. (As mother) But you look *terrible* in red. You know you don't look good in red.

*Fritz:* Are you aware of how much more alive you are when you play your mother? (Judy laughs.) Yah. Your voice at least has *some* kind of quality. Now comes the $64 question. How old are you?

*Judy:* Twenty-one.

*Fritz:* Twenty-one. And what do you need a mother for?

*Judy:* I don't need a mother!

*Fritz:* Tell her.

*Judy:* I don't need you. I *don't* need you.

*Fritz:* What does she answer?

*Judy:* (As mother) I know. But—You know we're there. Just in case of an emergency. You know where to come.

*Fritz:* Now go on writing the script.

*Judy:* (As self) But, in case of an emergency, I want to be able to do it myself, you know. I don't want to have to need you for an emergency. (As mother) Yeah, I know. But you know, just in case. If you need mo-o-o-ney. You know. Something like that (General laughter) (As self) But I don't need money. I'm doing all right by myself. And if I did need it, I'd find a way to get it.

*Fritz:*   Now you are always talking more or less defensively. How could you—If you don't need your mother, how come you don't get rid of her?

*Judy:*   I don't know how.

*Fritz:*   Now, I give you an ideal Fritz. Put him in that chair and ask him how to get rid of your mother. Here is your own psychiatrist.

*Judy:*   (Speaking to the imaginary Fritz in the other chair) Fritz, I've thought about this a long time, and I'm really hung up on my mother. And I think you can tell me how.

*Fritz:*   Now play him.

*Judy:*   (As Fritz, she waves an imaginary cigarette, flicking off imaginary ash. There is general laughter. She takes several drags—more laughter. Speaking as Fritz.) Make me your mother. I am your mother. What do you do to me? (She changes chairs; as Judy, she pounds the chair on which imaginary Fritz is sitting. She pounds and pummels it.)

*Fritz:*   What did you do now?

*Judy:*   I killed my mother. (There is general laughter.)

*Fritz:*   Yah? Okay, now play the dead mother. (Pause.) What do you experience as the dead mother?

*Judy:*   Pain.

*Fritz:*   Express it.

*Judy:*   (Agonized screaming and sobbing, over and over.)

*Fritz:*   Have you any idea what happened?

*Judy:*   I don't have an idea now. (Dorothy says something.)

*Fritz:*   (To Dorothy) Will you take this seat? (Dorothy takes the chair opposite Judy.)

*Dorothy:*   You still need your mother. Otherwise you wouldn't have felt so much pain that you killed her.

*Fritz:*   (To Dorothy) You see, you are thinking for her. And all this thinking for her helps to prevent her from growing.

156

*Dorothy:*   Right.

*Fritz:*   This is exactly what we're trying not to do. We're trying to frustrate our patients. We're trying to force them to develop their own potential, to learn to stand on their own feet. So we try to give as little support as possible. If she doesn't know what happened, I don't know. I can only fantasize. And I might give completely misleading suggestions. (Dorothy goes back to her seat. Fritz, to Judy) What do you feel now?

*Judy:*   I still feel—cut off.

*Fritz:*   You feel cut off. From what?

*Judy:*   From myself. I can't breathe.

*Fritz:*   Close your eyes and enter your body. Give us exact details how you prevent yourself from breathing. Can you take responsibility for what you are doing to yourself?

*Judy:*   I'm closing my throat.

*Fritz:*   Yah.

*Judy:*   I'm holding my stomach. Tightening my mouth. Knotting my stomach.

*Fritz:*   What are you doing to your stomach?

*Judy:*   Knotting it up.

*Fritz:*   Yah. Now, can you do all this—what you are doing to yourself—to your (Picture) mother? (Judy twists, squeezes, pummels, wrings her mother, making agonized noises.) Make more noises at it. (Judy cries, screams, pants.) What do you feel now?

*Judy:*   I feel better now. I feel like a witch.

*Fritz:*   Yah. Yah. Yah. Now, I make you a witch. What could you do to me? (Judy makes threatening gestures at Fritz.) (Picture) Enjoy being a witch? (Judy laughs, Judy explodes) Okay, that's as far as I want to go with this dream. I just want to say a bit more about—let's call it for the time being—the dream technique. In the historical context, it, so to say, derives its source from two other psychiatrists: one is Moreno and his psychodrama. The disadvantage of Moreno's Psychodrama is that he has to put in other people. And then the role is falsified by the uniqueness of the other person. If I let a person himself or herself create the different roles, then we know we are at home. The other part of the technique is Carl Rogers' feedback technique. But first, I have to say there is another difference between the Moreno technique and this one. Moreno usually confines himself to people. But there is so much invested in the objects. So if we make the objects alive—I can't go now into the relationship to the deadness of a person—again we have more material to assimilate. So the other person is Carl Rogers with his feedback technique. Only I don't use just sentences for feedback. I feed back the experience and make people listen to each other. There is no other choice—*fighting or listening*. If the U.N. would listen instead of fighting, we would have peace. *But who has ears? Who listens?*

## Polarities in Marriage*

In this film Fritz Perls demonstrates a couple of the features of Gestalt Therapy which was the psychotherapy developed by him. He recognized that each of us has within us opposite polarities, and we are not in touch with one of the opposites. Often we project the other one out there on to someone else. Fritz also saw that we invariably choose a marriage partner who represents whatever opposites or polarities we are not in touch with in ourselves.

So in this film he uses work with a husband and wife together, to demonstrate how he can put each in touch with the missing polarities in themselves and each other. And by working with the two, together they can use the combined energy of the two to achieve greater results.

*Madeleine:* I woke up. (Sniffing) When I was very small, I, it, didn't bother me. I was just happy to be swimming. I didn't care about not drinking the water. But as I grew older I got more and more resentful not to be able to drink the water.

*Fritz:* All right, this is as far as I want to go. Again, you see the same that we did before with the dreams. No interpretation. You know everything; you know much more than I do and all my interpretations would only mislead you. It's again, simply the question of learning, uncovering your true self.

* Aquarian Films

*Madeleine:*   Thank you.

*Bill:*   Um, I have a dream.

*Fritz:*   Yah, Don't move. What can you say about his posture?

*Bill:*   Pause, in a low voice, "I'm covering my genitals."

*Fritz:*   Yah. Can you tell this to the group? I'm covering my genitals.

*Bill:*   I'm covering my genitals.

*Fritz:*   Elaborate on this.

*Bill:*   Hmmm?

*Fritz:*   Elaborate on this. Again, let me remind you, we don't ask why in Gestalt therapy, we always ask how. We inquire about the structure and the best way to do it is to go into further detail.

*Bill:*   I guess I'm expecting a kick in the balls. And I'm probably trying to protect myself a bit.

*Fritz:*   Okay, Take the empty chair. And you're the enemy now. Bill, I want to kick you in the balls.

*Bill:*   Um, Bill, I want to kick you in the balls.

*Fritz:*   Now write the script between the kicker and the other.

*Bill:*   (Sigh) So what have you got against me? I mean, why do you feel so hostile?

*Bill* (Changed):   It's because you're being a bit of an ass, Bill. You're not really willing to open yourself up.

*Bill:*   If I open myself up, then I'd have no protection against you kicking me in the balls, would I?

*Bill* changed:   Why don't you just take your chances? Can't you?                ˙

*Fritz:*   Sit down again, and look around. I told you all looks, michega, craziness, inhibitions, are irrational fantasy. Let's check out your fantasy. Look around. Who was ready to kick you in the balls?

*Bill:*   No one I can see.

*Fritz:*   So what did you do, protect yourself for?

*Bill:*   (Laughing).

*Fritz:*   You saw ghosts. You saw your own ghost. Close your eyes. Now imagine kicking me in the balls. What do you experience then?

*Bill:*   Hurt.

*Fritz:*   You feel hurt?

*Bill:*   I feel, umm.

*Fritz:*   Come on. Don't give me that crap. How can you feel hurt if you kick me in the balls?

*Bill:*   I feel that, I feel that it's really not something I ought to do.

*Fritz:*   Yah.

*Bill:*   I imagine kicking you, I imagine you doubling up.

*Fritz:*   Yah.

*Bill:*   And I sort of see bruises and, I just see a lovely old man doubled up in pain.

*Fritz:*   Yah. Now play this old man doubling up in pain. I don't think you would sit on the chair. Now act it out. Ham it up. What do you feel now?

*Fritz:*   Now look at me. Do I comply with the picture of that man you just hit? So you kick, and kick me a thousand times in the balls, in fantasy. I'm still the same as I am. You can kill a person a thousand times in fantasy. This is what Socrates said. The difference between the good person and the bad person is that the good person does in fantasy what the bad person does in reality or in actuality. All right, you have a dream?

*Bill:*   It's a very short kind of a dream. But it's, recurring, the last few years. And I'm very simply flying. And I feel in a way that I'm soaring rather than flying. Soar, like a, like a bird. And I am flying, I don't know, perhaps, twenty feet off the ground, and I, just sort of, I just glide over the landscape and I tend to follow the contours of the landscape as I fly. And I see (Sigh) I see houses and I see streets, and churches and steeples and I see trees and I, I feel more, I feel very good when I'm soaring like this. I feel free. And that's about all there is to the dream.

*Fritz:*   So, play the landscape. And give us your story when you see Bill. Lie down. Be the landscape.

*Bill:*   And that, that's Bill flying. Zooming over my head.

*Fritz:*   Talk to Bill; Bill, you're above my head.

*Bill:*   Hello, Bill. I see you're out flying again today. Uh huh. You seem to enjoy it. You seem to enjoy flying above my head. I guess you feel pretty good when you're up there

**160**

and you can look down on us all here.

*Fritz:*   Say this again.

*Bill:*   I guess you feel pretty good when you can fly around up there and look down on us, on us all here.

*Fritz:*   And landscape, what does it make you feel, when you, Bill, looks down at you?

*Bill:*   Well, at first I feel—wow, it should be great to be able to fly and feel a bit, bit inferior and then I realize that, I realize that I'm solid, things grow out of me and . . .

*Fritz:*   Say this again. This is the message now.

*Bill:*   Things grow out of me and they don't grow out of something that just flies.

*Fritz:*   Okay, change roles, (Pause) No, Bill is not sitting, he is flying. Come on change roles.

*Bill:*   It's very free up here. The wind's whistling around my ears, and nothing to tie me down here. Ah, it's beautiful. Just floating—soaring. Things passing by. They're interesting from this sort of scale.

*Fritz:*   Try always to use the word you.

*Bill:*   You're interesting from, from up here. On the other hand, I'm not really involved with you. I just pass you by. I just pass you by.

*Fritz:*   Okay, there's another key sentence. Sit down. And say this sentence to each member of the audience.

*Bill:*   I just fly over and pass you by. And, and all I see is a few little shreds of you. And I fly over and just go past you and I never really get to know you, Mark. I just come by for a little while and then I'm gone. We never really, uh, we never really get there.

*Fritz:*   Do you get the message?

*Bill:*   Mmmmh.

*Fritz:*   Say this once more to her (his wife Ann).

*Bill:*   (sigh) I'm just flying by all the time. (pause, begins to cry) I never stop long enough to let it happen.

*Fritz:*   Get up. Talk to her. Like this.

*Bill:*   It doesn't matter because I'm here now. I, I think I'm going to stay awhile. And, uh, it's as free sitting down here as it is flying up there.

*Fritz:*   What's your response, Ann?

*Ann:*   I, I feel it isn't as, you know, it isn't as free down here as it is up there.

*Bill:*   And you don't even have to worry about that. Yeh, I know it isn't and what's the difference? For you.

*Fritz:*   Could we try something, Ann?

*Ann:*   Mmmh.

*Fritz:*   You change roles now. You play him and you take off and you're above us all. And you play Ann being down on the ground.

*Bill:*   Do you want to fly around?

*Ann:*   (Laugh) (Sniffling) I'm, uh, I'm flying like a bird up in the sky. (Sniff) I don't have any attachment to the ground at all. I'm just floating. I look down and I see you, on the ground. And, I feel like flying away. My, actually, I find it pretty tiring. I'm going to have to come down.

*Fritz:*   Now you respond as Ann. You respond as Ann. You're Ann now.

*Bill:*   I, I, uh, I like to see you soar, Bill. I know you enjoy it.

*Fritz:*   The angels call it the joy of heaven, the devil's torture of hell. Man calls it love. Well, we have a good example here of what always happens if things proceed properly. Finally all the conflicts, all the splits, come out in exact polarity. We had here the polarity of down—above. Having the feet on the ground or having the flights of fantasies. We have often the split. We had the split between top dog and under dog before. We haven't touched the tremendous importance between right and left but you see again and again, people find polarities and we can then find the centers of these polarities. This is one of the means of integration.

### Birth of a Composer*

*Ilana:*   I'm holding Fritz in my arms and I'm blowing smoke—smoke into your mouth, Fritz. Your face is right up against mine and—and that's like a statement, in the dream. You're there and our mouths, our mouths are together and I'm blowing the smoke in. Right after that there's an an-

* Media—Psych Corporation

162

nouncement, there's going to be a concert in front of a pool—there's going to be a big concert in front of the pool. And we go to the concert and there's a—and there's a girl conducting the orchestra. She's got long hair and she looks like one of the waitresses in the dining room. And she's conducting an overture and I'm sitting there—oh, boy, she's so crappy, and the overture is such a—it reminds me of camp when the conductor—we use to come like two violins and two flutes, one cello—eeeaak, you know, horrible, absolutely, with the cymbals and ludicrous, really ludicrous sounds. And she's conducting very serious and just like horrible sounds. I'm sitting there with a smirk on my face and, and saying like you know whoever is near me, "Oh, boy, that's so shitty, she's so shitty." And I walk away, I walk away I walk away from her conducting and the sounds—oh yeah, NBC and CBS are recording this, and that even gets me more furious and I walk away and my cousin comes up to me—Frank's cousin actually—and she says, she says "You know, Ilana, I think I'm going to take up conducting." And I look at her and, you know, I hate her, but what I say with a big smile is "Oh, that's wonderful, you know, that ought to be very exciting." And she says, "But I wouldn't like to have someone laughing in the audience at *me*." And I say some crazy like—(pause)

*Fritz:*   What do you experience right now?

*Ilana:*   Like being, like being told, "I wouldn't like to have someone laughing in the audience like—in the audience at me.

*Fritz:*   Say this sentence again.

*Ilana:*   I wouldn't like to have someone laughing in the audience at *me.*

*Fritz:*   Say this to the group.

*Ilana:*   I wouldn't like to have someone in the audience laughing at me. (Pause). My breathing is like very jumpy and—

*Fritz:*   Enter your body.

*Ilana:*   Yeah—my hands are, are wet and clammy, which, you know disgusts me. I don't like them like that. My breathing is like lumpy, goes bu, bu, bu. I felt vicious.

*Fritz:*   Now go back to the dream—to us and say one

more of this sentence, "I don't want anyone —"

*Ilana:* I wouldn't like anybody here in the audience laughing at me. (Loudly!)

*Fritz:* So get back to your body.

*Ilana:* Little better. Ah. Still shaky, heart pounding fast, but I feel better, I can take deeper breaths, they're not so shallow, they're not like that.

*Fritz:* Ilana, come back to the sentences.

*Ilana:* Was there a sentence?

*Fritz:* That sentence.

*Ilana:* I wouldn't like anybody in the audience laughing at *me!* (Pause)

*Fritz:* Afraid?

*Ilana:* It's there, it's there. How—ugh, how dare you laugh at me, how dare you laugh at me, while I'm conducting?

*Fritz:* So change seats, play the person who laughs.

*Ilana:* Okay, She's so funny, she's standing up there and conducting two violins and four tympanis, twenty flutes, you know, she thinks she's good, she's really conducting up there, conducting an orchestra, she's, see she doesn't even, it's so shitty—and she just stays up there and conducts. God, I wouldn't be found dead up there. You get me at least an eight piece orchestra. God, what shit.

(changes seats)

—Well you come on up here and conduct then, you brave, brave thing. That really got me when she said woman, and a woman, too, up there. That really—I don't want people in the audience laughing at me. You shit, you don't even know what it sounds like and you're criticizing me. You're sitting out there."

(changes seats)

—It's okay, she's got her back to me, that's you know, I can kep doing that 'cause, you see, she's telling you, telling everybody that she's a shit. She can't see me, her back is to me. How can she conduct that sound? Besides, she's, she's a waitress, she's a waitress and she gets up there and waves her arms around. You know.

*Fritz:* Okay, now be this orchestra.

*Ilana:* Oh, shit, everyone laughs. You got music? (Starts to move around and do something)

*Fritz:* No no, no no no, I want that you be that orchestra.

*Ilana:* That orchestra, right, that's not the orchestra. That's the eighty piecer and they're smucks too. (Everyone begins to laugh). She's got, she's got, like that—

*Fritz:* I am the orchestra.

*Ilana:* I am the orchestra.

*Fritz:* Four tympanis.

*Ilana:* Yeah, and I've been just put together for this stupid concert in front of a pool, everyone is around the lawn and, it's so ridiculous and we doing an overture and we're doing an overture, and I'm four tympanis, and I'm two cymbals, and (She does a pantomime of the instruments and everyone is laughing) twenty flutes, playing left hand, right hand, and two violins and one cello. I like a cello. And this chick, like she serves lunches over there, and she's conducting and this is the stupidest—

*Fritz:* She's conducting me.

*Ilana:* Yeah, oh yeah, she's conducting me and this is the stupidest sound, Oh, I forgot, about twelve clarinets (She begins vocalization of sounds of the orchestra, much laughing from the group) Schreech, squack, scratch . . . etc. and it's horrible, I'm horrible and I'm a horrible sound. And people are listening to this. Oh, you're listening to me seriously. Everyone is nodding. I'm making an ass of everybody. I'm so shitty, and they all think I'm so great and I'm so shitty. My God, how people are fooled. I'm such a shit. Yeah. (Pause) I felt good doing that, real good. (Pause) So I'm running away from this cousin of mine.

*Fritz:* Wait a minute. Let's come back to this.

*Ilana:* Okay, and I see everybody very clearly. Not too close, but like like I'm viewing them next to me. I'm looking at you. I see you clearly but I'm looking at you, I'm not there, like audience, you're there; I'm here.

(changes tone of voice) Oh, isn't this just beautiful, it's just first class.

*Fritz:* This is to her, I feel just beautiful and the orchestra . . .

*Ilana:* Oh, you're just beautiful, first class. The best I've heard in months, this is just really, this is really, this is really music. What an orchestra! You are just really something. Really balanced. Heavy on the winds, so it's not too schmaltzy, you know. Strings tend to make it too mushy, you really have hit on a new sound.

*Fritz:* Say this again.

*Ilana:* You've hit on a new sound.

*Fritz:* Again.

*Ilana:* You've hit on a new sound.

*Fritz:* Okay, now come back and write a piece for this orchestra.

*Ilana:* Write a piece for this orchestra?

*Fritz:* Yah, this is your homework, without ridiculing it.

*Ilana:* Okay.

*Fritz:* Any idea what you're upset about.

*Ilana:* (Long pause) I have feelings, I have feelings, you know, I have ideas. I'd use a percussions a lot 'cause I've got four tympany and two cymbals and I would use the flutes, since I have so many flutes, (Sings a melody) like bagpipes, all the time (sings) and have a group of flutes weave around it, weave around that like an obligatto, you know, a bass, a grand bass going, and the drums, four of them might go (sings another melody) I've two violins. I'll only use one. Forgive me, Abe, I—I hear in a dream, I heard this tune (sings). No, that's not the cello, I—(sings the melody and starts crying).

## Treatment with Gestalt Therapy

### Relentless Greed*

*Dianne:* (Sitting in the chair next to Dr. Perls) My feet are on the floor, and my back on the cushion, and holding back with my arms. And you, (laughing) your shining face. And your toes, and silver (on Dr. Perls necklace) shining.

*Media—Psych Corporation

166

*Fritz:* Can you instead of and, and, and, and, instead of this mishmosh say period after each sentence?

*Dianne:* I'm aware of the blue on your shirt—period. I'm aware of the curl—period, and the microphone—period.

*Fritz:* Do me a favor, just stick with the simple sentence, "Now I discover." You may finally start to discover, but first at least let's hold on to the sentence.

*Dianne:* Now I discover—my leg—Now I discover—my arms—period. Now I discover the noise—period. Now I discover the beating in my heart, period. Now I discover my elbows—period. Now I discover your hand, (she raises her voice.) period. Now I discover my voice—period.

*Fritz:* You recovered it.

*Dianne:* Now I discover my discomfort, period. Now I discover the ant—period. (Laughing) The shadow—period. The shine on your head—period.

*Fritz:* How come it takes you such a long time to get your period? (The group laughs.)

*Dianne:* Birth control pills.

*Fritz:* You see, you say the word period. You wait awhile and then dutifully you put it on, but the sentence is still not yet a complete statement. It's still not yet a Gestalt. It's still open.

*Dianne:* Now I discover your mouth, period.

*Fritz:* Now, the sadness of that statement flew into the word period.

*Dianne:* Now I discover your wiping your nose —period. And your smile—period. And that cast—period. (laughing) And my feet—period. My toe and my other toes—period. Cigarette—period.

*Fritz:* I'm afraid I have to give an interpretation. It is as if you can't stand to have your mouth empty. It always has to be filled.

*Dianne:* That's true. (laughing) But of what? Now I discover my white leg. (sighing). I discover my sigh, my confusion—period. Now I discover that I feel like hiding, period.

*Fritz:* Okay, now try to differentiate when you discover something and when something discovers you—surprises you.

*Dianne:* Between when something discovers me and when I discover? (She sighs.) Now I discover Dick—period. (Dick is the cinematographer who is filming.)

*Fritz:* Say this again.

*Dianne:* Now I discover Dick—period.

*Fritz:* Again.

*Dianne:* (With increasing anxiety) Now I discover Dick—period.

*Fritz:* Again.

*Dianne:* Now I discover Dick—period. (She begins to cry.) Now I discover Dick—period.

*Fritz:* Okay, now what do you experience?

*Dianne:* (She sighs) A welling-up of emotion and then cutting off and then losing the now, and judging.

*Fritz:* Okay, now close your eyes. You said you discovered Dick, can you tell me what you discovered?

*Dianne:* His white shirt, and his looking at me, (crying) and my need, my need for contact, (Sighing, crying) I'm discovering how much I hold back my feelings. Now I discover that I am judging my crying. I am judging whether or not it is real.

*Fritz:* So go back to Dick.

*Dianne:* (Breathing heavily, crying)

*Fritz:* Close your eyes and go away again.

*Dianne:* I discover my breathing. My mouth is dry, that my mouth is empty. (She laughs and her laughter turns to sobbing.) My mouth is empty. I feel a need to fill my mouth up.

*Fritz:* Okay, open your eyes. Open your eyes. Swallow Dick up.

*Dianne:* (She sobs and her crying turns to laughter.)

## The Treatment of Stuttering*

*Fritz:* Your first name is . . . ?

*Fred:* Fred.

*Fritz:* Fred?

*Fred:* Yes, Fred Vaughn.

*Media—Psych Corporation

*Fritz:*   What do you experience?

*Dick:*   Do you want to sit in the other chair so that you can be seen on the camera? (Dick moves from one seat to another.)

*Fritz:*   What do you experience, Fred?

*Fred:*   Right now?

*Fritz:*   Yeah.

*Fred:*   All of this—Like it feels like—pulsating in my arms and my chest. And I feel like I've been out of breath.

*Fritz:*   Close your eyes. And withdraw into yourself. Get in touch with all your symptoms. So what do you experience?

*Fred:*   I feel like I'm breathing really heavy. I don't know why, though. My breathing's a little jerky. I still feel the pulsating all through my chest and through my forehead. This seems to die down a little bit as I talk.

*Fritz:*   If you can integrate attention and awareness, then you'll see what will happen. Just keep your full attention on whatever you are aware of. Get in touch with your experience.

*Fred:*   Everything that I was aware of at first seems to be dying down. I—I can hardly feel my heart beat anymore.

Fritz:   I want you to get over your stage fright. Let's look at our audience. How do you experience your audience?

*Fred:*   Pretty much just faces, a bunch of color, speechless, quiet.

*Fritz:*   So go back to your other experiences.

*Fred:*   Well, I—I f-feel my heart starting to go f-f-f-f-faster again.

*Fritz:*   Okay, withdraw into yourself and tend to your symptoms. (pause) Please don't change what you are doing with your right hand. Describe what you are doing with your right hand.

*Fred:*   I'm taking my thumb and rubbing it with the tip of my forefinger of my left hand.

*Fritz:*   Can you let your right hand talk to the left hand? Give it something to say. Invent some dialogue between your right hand and your left hand.

*Fred:*   (Stuttering) The left hand is rubbing the ball, the tip of the right hand.

*Fritz:* Play your right hand. "I am rubbing—"

*Fred:* Oh, I see.

*Fritz:* *Your* ball.

*Fred:* (Stuttering) I am rubbing your ball in order to make it feel better. It doesn't feel better.

*Fritz:* I noticed that you were stammering. Could you exaggerate the stammering?

*Fred:* T-t-t-t-t-t-t-t-t-t-t-t-t-t, d-d-d-d-d-d-d-d-d-do.

*Fritz:* What do you feel in your throat? What do you feel in your throat?

*Fred:* Oh, a blocking, a fullness, going up into the palatal area. Right now I feel a real tightness going on.

*Fritz:* Let's see if we can do a shortcut. Will you come to me, take my arm and with both hands, as if my arm was your throat, begin to choke me.

*Fred:* Choke it as if it was my throat.

*Fritz:* Yeah. And talk to me at the same time: "I'm going to choke you to death."

*Fred:* I'm going to choke you to death so you can't talk anymore.

*Fritz:* Go ahead.

*Fred:* I'm going to squeeze and just push it so hard that you won't be able to breathe. Then you won't be able to do anything.

*Fritz:* So what happened to your stammering?

*Fred:* I didn't think about it.

*Fritz:* Exactly, because you killed me instead of yourself. You choked me instead of yourself. Say this to you: "Fred, I'm going to throttle you so that you won't be able to talk."

*Fred:* Fred, I'm going to throttle you so that you cannot talk.

*Fritz:* Again.

*Fred:* Fred, I am going to throttle you so that you cannot talk.

*Fritz:* Put all of you into it.

*Fred:* Fred, I'm going to throttle you so you can't talk. (yelling)

*Fritz:* Again.

*Fred:* Fred, I'm going to throttle you so you can't talk,

you son of a bitch. (yelling)

*Fritz:*   Now, get your whole self, get your whole anger into it.

*Fred:*   Fred, I'm going to throttle you so you can't talk. (Yelling louder.)

*Fritz:*   Okay, thank you. That's how you've got to get rid of your stuttering. That's how you've got to do it.

*Fred:*   To get angry?

*Fritz:*   Is there anyone in the audience you want to throttle?


## Grief by Tova

*Tova:*   I'm in my parent's house, where I lived until I left home. And my Daddy and she are standing on a small balcony that's out of my room. I'm in the room and I watch them stand there leaning against the railing, talking, or playing. And all of a sudden my Daddy does some unexpected movement and he falls over the railing. At this moment I wake up all excited and worried. It took me a few minutes after I woke up to calm down. That's the whole dream.

*Fritz:*   What have you against David?

*Tova:*   My Daddy?

*Fritz:*   Yes.

*Tova:*   What have I against my Daddy?

*Fritz:*   You have to go over, from the beginning.

*Tova:*   What do I have against you? I love you very much.

*Fritz:*   I believe you.

*Tova:*   You're very sweet and charming. What do I have against you? What do I have against you? (Changing chairs.) Right now you don't have anything against me. So when do I hurt you? Sometimes when I, when I, when I don't want to do what you tell me to do. And if it doesn't seem to be very important, all of a sudden you get so mad and you scare me. I can see the scared look on your face and there's nothing I can do against it. If—

*Fritz:*   Hold—

*Tova:* It's—

*Fritz:* Let's—

*Tova:* It's—

*Fritz:* Say to yourself, look and control, then say I'm controlling it and if I can't control somebody I get mad.

*Tova:* I'm controlling it and if I can't control somebody I get very mad. It's still too general for me. When I have —When I have it on my mind that I want you to do something, then its very important to me at that moment to do something. I can't stand it if you refuse to do it. I won't accept it and then I'll make you do it. So I'm mad at you, so I'll be mad at you. (Changes Chairs) Okay, it's all right for you to be mad at me. Oh, it's all right as long as I say that it is all right, as long as I can accept it, but there's a limit. If I can't accept you when you are mad then I'll let you know.

*Fritz:* Okay, be your parent's apartment now.

*Tova:* (Crying) Leave me to the dream. (Pause crying), I don't want to. I don't want to be there. Still loaded with things I want to forget.

*Fritz:* Such as?

*Tova:* The sad atmosphere. There's my mother, the way it looked, I didn't like the way it looked. The furniture in it, it was drab and small. I keep seeing my parents' room and my mother. I resist going into the room.

*Fritz:* So be the room.

*Tova:* I'll be the bookcase thing, the round table and a mirror, three wooden chairs, and a wooden cupboard with drawers and—and parts where you hang clothes, a couch that opens up into a bed, my mother's small table. Oh, so much funiture there is hardly any room to move in.

*Fritz:* Say this, I am.

*Tova:* I am stuffed, I am so cluttered up, there isn't much open space in me. All the things that I include are not good looking. They're old pieces of furniture, they don't fit together at all. Each one comes from a different time. But it all serves a certain function; it all serves a certain purpose. The people who live in me need each one of these things and it's just that there isn't a lot of space to put it, there isn't any more space. I have a nice big window, very big window brings the street in. When you—when you stand at my window you can really be more in the street than in me. You can watch the people go by, you can, you get fresh air.

*Fritz:*   So be Tova again.

*Tova:*   The strongest memory from my—from this room is my mother lying dead on the couch. (Crying.)

*Fritz:*   Go to her, go to her.

*Tova:*   She looks awful.

*Fritz:*   Say *you* to her.

*Tova:*   You look awful and this dumb doctor is just sitting there not doing anything, and I—

*Fritz:*   You feel helpless?

*Tova:*   No, I just feel sad. And I say to him, "What has to be done?" and he says, "It's too late," And so I go up to you and shut your eyes and hug you and kiss you and say goodbye (sobbing). That's the only way I remember you now. That's the only memory I carry. I can't see your face. I only see you lying there on the couch looking at me (sobs). And after I say good-bye I pull the blankets over you, and, and I get rid of the doctor, I get rid of everybody anybody who's ever there (sob). All of a sudden, no warning nothing. And then my father comes in, and I go to him—and I hug him and I tell him that mother is gone (pause) and I try to comfort him.

*Fritz:*   What does he say?

*Tova:*   You're very good, he doesn't know what to do—he's shocked. And in order not to, collapse, he starts, he starts taking care of procedures and things like that, so that there is something to do, since it's too late to do anything.

*Fritz:*   Tova, you trust me don't you?

*Tova:*   Yes.

*Fritz:*   Okay, I have to ask you to do this scene all over again once more. (Pauses) She is on the couch dead, the doctor is just standing there, go back once more.

*Tova:*   (Changing seats) I walk into the room—and I was already anxious because I was walking in the street toward the house, and a neighbor told me that my mother doesn't feel well and it made me panicky because how would she know that my mother doesn't feel well? Mother doesn't feel well often but nobody knows about it. (Pause) Do I have to go into it again?

*Fritz:* Your neighbor just told you mother doesn't feel well. What is there before you go in? What happens then?

*Tova:* I start running from that point. It was two houses away from home.

*Fritz:* Yah.

*Tova:* And I run as fast as I can—because I realize that something is terribly wrong if, if this lady knows that my mother doesn't feel well, and I mean she doesn't even live in the same house.

*Fritz:* How do you get through the door?

*Tova:* The door is open. I just—I just run into the house, open the door, run in the room—and I see this man sitting on the chair, with no one near him. And another neighbor tells me he is a doctor, then I turn and I see my mother (sobbing) she's—I can tell that she's unconscious, and she looks awful and I turn to the doctor and I say "What can I do?" (sobbing) and he says it's too late. And I go up (sobbing loudly) and I, and I close her eyes and I push her jaw so her mouth would be shut and I—I kissed and hugged her (sobbing) and I pull the blanket over her. (Sobbing more) I talk to the doctor some more. I ask him what happened. And he said that when he came it was too late. That when he came she was dead already so he didn't know what it was what she died from. He makes me mad. I—I can't—I can't stand it (Pause), I haven't been to that place for a long time, either.

*Fritz:* I'm sorry, Tova, but you've got to go through it once more.

*Tova:* What kind of a torture is that?

*Fritz:* It will help you.

*Tova:* (Sobbing) I don't want to do it over and over again.

*Fritz:* Is there anything about her death that you torture yourself about.

*Tova:* I don't think so. The only thing is I sometimes have fantasy—I have dreams after that that she was sick so I could take care of her. I didn't have a chance to do anything. But I haven't had them in a long time. It was just right after she died. And I still feel that I didn't have a chance to do things for her.

*Fritz:*  Can you try she didn't give you a chance?

*Tova:*  Because I'm so late from school?

*Fritz:*  Yeah, without giving you a warning.

*Tova:*  But all of a sudden we went out to the street in the morning and I went on my way and I came back at lunch time and you were gone. (Pause continues whispering) It was such a shock.

*Fritz:*  Try this for size, "How could you do this to me?"

*Tova:*  How could you do that to me? How could you do that to me? (pause) I feel the opposite, Fritz.

*Fritz:*  Yeah?

*Tova:*  I feel that she did me a lot of good by going away just then.

*Fritz:*  Uh huh, Say this to her then.

*Tova:*  God. It's hard to tell you, but I feel that it was good for me to go along by myself. (Sobbing) To be on my own from then on. (Long pause) I didn't know it then, when it happened, but now I feel that it made life easier for me. Anyway just then. (long pause). All of a sudden as a result I took myself in my own hands and started doing things, that I felt I ought to have done. (Pause) And you, if you had stayed around I would have just—let things slip. I wouldn't have taken a step. That way it was good for me that you'd gone, that you left. (Pause) I don't even miss you very often any more. I haven't dreamed about you in years. (In a whisper) I feel very hot.

*Fritz:*  Okay, withdraw into yourself.

*Tova:*  (She closes her eyes and breathes deeply.)

*Fritz:*  (After awhile) What's in your belly?

*Tova:*  I find it hard to relax but now it's relaxing.

*Fritz:*  Come back to us, especially to Shima (her husband). (Tova cries after this and she goes and embraces him and then returns to the hot seat).

*Fritz:*  How do you feel about having gone back?

*Tova:*  Strange, I've been in that room so many times before, and right now—this feels to me like one more time. But there was no terror this time and there used to be.

*Fritz:*  You work something through.

*Tova:*  (Interrupts) I didn't hear what you said.

*Fritz:*  I said if you work something through, I think,

shocking them, appreciation of whatever it is.

*Tova:*   Except that I don't feel anything new in what is happening. I haven't discovered, I have never expressed myself in this way. (Laughs).

*Fritz:*   How about again?

*Tova:*   Fritz, I trust you and I know that what I feel at this moment is not what I'm going to feel tomorrow and I trust you that I'm going to feel better. I really do. (Long pause)

*Fritz:*   Again, in many instances, we must go over this again and again, there are always details left out. Then we get the Gestalt disclosure if it's in a remote part. But then, we get entry into a much more rational appreciation. But there's still something that can *stop my knowing* some kind of ability of controlling that.

*Tova:*   I don't know. (Pause) I do. I think I do now.

*Fritz:*   You see, you look upon it still as how did it feel for you. It's not affecting you; you're up, you will see how you manipulate it rather than it destroying you.

*Tova:*   Well, I don't see that either. That's what I started being like that. I understand. I had a first glimpse of it. (long pause) It's easy with my father when I'm looking at it.

*Fritz:*   I give you one more tip. One of your main means of manipulating is out-waiting—out-waiting. If I wait long enough you come across, you can speak.


## Grief and Pseudo-Grief*

*Fritz:*   You're not ready to realize what you are doing to him.

*Nancy:*   I'm still pissed off at you.

*Fritz:*   You're going back again.

*Nancy:*   I don't have to take this. I don't have to take it from anybody here, either.

*Fritz:*   You're not supposed to check up. Okay, who else?

* Media—Psych Corporation

*Nancy:* I've had two dreams lately and in the end both concern my father. One of them is at our house and there's a group of relatives over and, Fritz, you're in the dream. At the end we asked you about Gestalt Therapy and you say to my father, "That is a sick lamp." My father is sitting; it is also a death symbol. You can talk to the death symbol and then I don't remember what happens until—then my father says something like "I realize I got out of this and want you to record my voice again."

*Fritz:* You are the only one when I have been nasty.

*Nancy:* Thank you, Fritz.

*Fritz:* I have been nasty.

*Nancy:* Okay, you're a bit too long.

*Nancy:* Why don't you shut up? (shattered) I am I guess I'm afraid if I am a bitch people will reject me and won't like me. You know I have got something, I am sick and tired you sit and giggle every goddam time.

*Fritz:* I love you.

*Nancy:* This man is a bitch.

*Fritz:* I feel alive.

*Nancy:* And you look like a devil biting your lip. Neville, Neville, the Devil. And, Ed, you really bug me. All I see is you really don't care.

*Fritz:* And I know there is more.

*Nancy:* I fantasize about her. I project all my inadequacies on everyone. You make me feel stupid. You make me feel like a GLA.

*Fritz:* If you can say something nice to me.

*Nancy:* I feel stupid. I am sick and tired of you, seeing you so goddamn bored every time I am up here.

*Fritz:* Sorry about yourself?

*Nancy:* Can't you be nice?

*Fritz:* If you comply.

*Nancy:* I am not going to be nasty. Who do you think I am? I'm not a puppet on a string.

*Fritz:* Oh, yes, you are.

*Nancy:* Yes, I am, goddam it, half the time! (laughing).

*Fritz:* Talk, be yourself.

*Nancy:* Can't you be nice? If you come, I am not going to be nasty. Just who do you think I am? I'm not a puppet.

*Fritz:*   Yes, you are.

*Nancy:*   Damn right I am!

*Fritz:*   Be a nasty puppet.

*Nancy:*   I am not going to be nasty to anybody. We're all here together.

*Fritz:*   You told me. You are a ham also.

*Nancy:*   That pissed me off.

*Fritz:*   Ham also?

*Nancy:*   What really pissed me off was right after you both talked about internal tradition all you care about is dollars and cents.

*Fritz:*   In Israel yet.

*Nancy:*   What if—fuck what they are saying.

*Fritz:*   What, what about—shattered—

*Nancy:*   Well, that's okay too. In Istanbul, worldwide Fritz. The United States isn't big enough for you.

*Fritz:*   No, it's not.

*Nancy:*   That's not nasty, necessarily you are a budding Jewish mother.

*Fritz:*   I am more.

*Nancy:*   The United States is not good enough for you. You had got nothing but yenta around you. You are nothing but a yenta yourself. Oivay Fritz. If your mother could only see you now. You are the doctor I wanted for a son, my therapist. The doctor I wanted for a son. Bigger than Ford. Now I feel heady.

*Fritz:*   Now do it with father.

*Nancy:*   I'd rather do my mother.

*Fritz:*   No, no, father, do your father. (up to this time Nancy had been joking and laughing; sometimes really angry, but she suddenly at this point breaks into shrieks and uncontrollable sobbing.

*Nancy:*   Daddy, Daddy, now can't you grow up? You're forty-six years old and you haven't grown up yet. Can't you stand up to mother at all? I want you to be a man.

*Fritz:*   Say this again.

*Nancy:*   I want you to be a man, Daddy, but you're not. You're not. Please be a man. You already died and you can't be any more. You are like a hard working mule. You worked all your life to give us things. You're not strong. You're not strong. I want you to grow up. I always wanted you to protect me and you never could. (Sobbing). You were never even around that much. You were always working and getting us things. I knew you loved me but it wasn't enough. You were so weak. You couldn't stand up to mother, (crying). Daddy, I wish you were here. I don't want you to be dead. You can't come back. I wanted to see you strong all my life. But you just stood by. You didn't even know I was there half of the time. You just blinded yourself to everything. You won't take responsibility. You spend you time getting money. You're gentle but it was weakness. You never got mad, you never stood up.

*Fritz:* Can you say he never protected you from mother?

*Nancy:* You never protected me from mother. You never knew what was going on. You were so blind. You wanted to think everything was okay, but you didn't even believe me when I told you what she did to me, but she did. Even when I told you what she did. You just said she couldn't do those things, but she did. She even choked me once and you wouldn't believe me. You were so goddam blind. Well, I wasn't happy like you think. It's too late now. You're dead and gone. I want you back. Yet it wasn't all bad. You led at times.

*Fritz:* Okay, that's enough, come back to us.

*Nancy:* (She tries to calm herself but almost starts sobbing again).

*Fritz:* Go back to your father.

*Nancy:* I don't feel well, you're dead. Oh, Daddy, I keep seeing you when I got back from school with the rabbi next to you. You waited for me all day long. I told you I loved you and I do. I really love you, Daddy (sobbing). I love you, I love you, Daddy. I love you, I love you. I want you to believe me, I really do. I love you, Daddy. I never felt that you believed me. But I do. I really love you.

*Fritz:* Now I believe you.

*Nancy:* I do. I love you. (calming herself, she begins to breathe deeply).

*Fritz:* So go into your breathing now; stay with your breathing.

*Nancy:* (Breathing deeply). Ahh. Ahh. I feel free.

*Fritz:* (handing her a kleenex) Say this to us.

*Nancy:* I feel free. (looking up) I feel my breath down here.

## The Mini-Satori*

*Fritz:* (voice over) In Zen, the aim is called enlightment or Satori. It means the waking up from the trance of Maya, of the unreality of our thinking. We are not generally aware of living completely and eternally in a trance, mostly in a verbal trance, in prejudices, inhibitions and so on. When we wake up from this trance, we call this in therapy the little-awakening, a mini-satori. The great Satori, the final waking up, the final enlightenment, is rare. But, quite frequently, we find a patient having a mini-satori, waking up, and then sliding back into a minor trance. Here, in the following short film, we have an exquisite little example of a deep trance, a kind of depersonalization, to a kind of waking up to coming out of this trance and seeing the world clearly, brightly and existent.

(Muriel, a woman in her mid-thirties, is a participant in a month-long workshop at Big Sur's Esalen Institute. Prior to this session, she had worked several times with Dr. Perls. On this occasion, she walked quietly to the hot seat, looked at each group member and then sat down. The workshop room became extremely quiet and devoid of the usual on-going shuffle of papers, ashtrays and the like. It seemed as though something super-natural in nature was present.)

*Muriel:* I want to have you around so I can kind of be with you and sit in the hot seat when I get nervy enough and so you can cure everybody—I just feel numb.

*Fritz:* Enter your numbness. (He touches her hand.)

*Muriel:* That made it less, right away. It's just very very heavy—especially on my face—and like some thick stuff is attached to me, around my face. And now is widening out. Ah. Oh, I'm not numb anymore.

* Media—Psych Corporation

*Fritz:*   The following is an experiment. I have no idea whether we're on the right track or not. Would you say good-bye to your youth?

*Muriel:*   I feel like I'm in it now. I immediately see myself as about 8 years old.

*Fritz:*   Could you say good-bye to the 8-year-old girl?

*Muriel:*   Are you really going away? Yeah, she says yeah, and she's turning around and walking away. Just fading out, right under Steve's sock.

*Fritz:*   Go back to the mirror. Can you say goodbye to that person?

*Muriel:*   I don't know that person.

*Fritz:*   Talk to it. Is it she or he?

*Muriel:*   She, it's me!

*Fritz:*   Well, first you have to make her acquaintance.

*Muriel:*   I don't really, do I?

*Fritz:*   Yes.

*Muriel:*   Well, she's just there in the mirror.

*Fritz:*   Talk to her.

*Muriel:*   Who are you? I've never seen you before. I don't recognize you. I don't feel like—I don't feel like I know you—I've never seen you before. Your eyes don't look like that usually.

*Fritz:*   What do her eyes look like now?

*Muriel:*   Well, they're brown, they're my eyes. They're brown and they're open. And, and there's a little sparkle in each one of them which is about one-twentieth the size of what I usually see in the mirror and then there's like a dead spot in each one—like that.

*Fritz:*   Now change seats. (Muriel moves to a chair which is directly in front of her and faces the hot seat.)

*Muriel:*   There. She doesn't say anything. She just looks and her expressions don't change.

*Fritz:*   Give her a voice.

*Muriel:*   Okay.

*Fritz:*   I don't believe this, "I don't say a word."

*Muriel:*   Okay, okay, I don't say anything. I'm just—I'm here looking out at you—looking out at you and I don't feel any life in me. And—and—and those two little sparks that you see in my eyes, that's just the light from outside, that doesn't come from me. (She moves back to the hot seat) Well, where did you come from? You know I'm not like that and, and you're my reflection, in the mirror. So—

*Fritz:*   Say this once more, "I'm not like that."

*Muriel:*   I'm not like that.

*Fritz:*   Again.

*Muriel:*   I'm not like that.

*Fritz:*   Again.

*Muriel:*   I'm not like that!

*Fritz:*   Again.

*Muriel:*   You're not *me.*

*Fritz:*   Again.

*Muriel:*   I'm not like that!

*Fritz:*   Again.

*Muriel:*   And I'm not.

*Fritz:*   Your voice becomes real. So be her again.

*Muriel:*   (moves to the other chair) So who's making the reflection in the mirror? Ha, ha, ha, that's you, cookie. (She moves back to the hot seat) I have no answer for you. That's got to be so—you're my reflection.

*Fritz:*   Say this to the group.

*Muriel:*   That's got to be so—you're my reflection?

*Fritz:*   Yes.

*Muriel:*   That's got to be so—you're my reflection. That's got to be so—you're my reflection. That's got to be so—you're my reflection. That's got to be so—you're my reflection. Well.

*Fritz:*   So, what do you actually experience?

*Muriel:*   Well, I feel like the top half is wanting to move and like there's blood in there.

*Fritz:*   Move it, a little. (Muriel begins to move the top half of her body in a swaying motion) a little bit more.

*Muriel:*   (Sweating) Wow, there's air in here, I feel the air. That's nice. Wow, where have I been?

*Fritz:*   Where *have* you been?

*Muriel:*   I don't know.

*Fritz:*   When you came to this seat you were in a trance; you weren't here.

*Muriel:*   Crazy.

*Fritz:* Yes, out of this world.

*Muriel:* Crazy.

*Fritz:* See?

*Muriel:* Sure, I just remembered Abe did the hypnotizing thing at the massage class yesterday.

*Fritz:* Back into a trance?

*Muriel:* Yea, right.

*Fritz:* Okay, go back to your trance.

*Muriel:* Well, now I feel all this motion, in my head and down my neck—all this motion.

*Fritz:* It's so difficult to try to return.

*Muriel:* Yes . . .

## The Demon*

*Fritz:* Now this is a very interesting film seen from the point of view of the demon. Of a possession by somebody else. The trouble here is that the demon doesn't appear as part of Neville but as a projection, as a persecution. Neville feels that he is persecuted by the demon. As always in Gestalt therapy, we let the patient identify himself with the different roles, with the different projections thereby taking back what is really his own. Now there is one point in the film where you might not understand what I was doing. I suddenly called in his mother. I had my good reasons because his whole previous therapy centered around his hatred for his mother. With the help of understanding him as the demon, we also understand that here and now he could really take the first steps in getting even with his mother.

*Neville:* (Neville is sitting next to Dr. Perls and clutching the arms of his chair) I, I, I, I feel—I, I'm being choked.

*Fritz:* Yes, now say this, I—I am the hands.

*Neville:* The hand.

*Fritz:* I am the choking hand.

*Neville:* I am the choking hand, but I'm attached to long arms. My fingers are long.

* Audiotape transcription, courtesy of John Stevens.

*Fritz:*   Talk to the group.

*Neville:*   And they're clawing, I have claws. I'm gonna choke you. (Loses control and begins screaming) I'm gonna choke you. (Screams and begins sobbing) I won't let you breathe.

*Fritz:*   Say this to somebody here, I won't let you breathe.

*Neville:*   (Looking at a man nearby) I won't let you breathe! (sobbing) I won't let you breathe, goddamn you! (Neville attacks him with his fists).

*Fritz:*   Hey, hey, hey, stop it, (Neville is restrained). That's another problem.

*Neville:*   (Crying and sobbing.)

*Fritz:*   Keep your eyes closed go down to the plunger, yeah, all alone, look out at the waves. (The plunger is the Esalen baths)

*Neville:*   I—I feel small and constricted.

*Fritz:*   Not yet, let—let your nightmare wait a bit. Open your eyes, and look at us with your own eyes, not with the eyes of the demon.

*Neville:*   I—I see you all but, there is a little mist between us.

*Fritz:*   Of course, of course. You're not with us. You're still with the demon. So tell us more about your demon.

*Neville:*   My demon, I am the demon. I—I hover over Neville—all the time. I'm waiting, just in case you make a move. I'm there to stop you and frighten you. If the hands, if my hands aren't sufficient, I bring my eyes to help me do the job.

*Fritz:*   Okay, now come back to us and and take someone here again, instead of Neville, do it to us.

*Neville:*   June, I'm your demon. I want to take you and I want to squeeze every breath of air out of you. And I'll stare at you as it's being done and I'll stare at you and you'll be so frightened you won't know what's happening to you. It will be the most horrible way you could imagine of going. My claws will sink into your neck.

*Fritz:*   What do you feel when you are the demon?

*Neville:*   Like a demon.

184

*Fritz:*  Do you feel any power?

*Neville:*  My hands. Yeah, I do feel power. It's very frightening.

*Fritz:*  Sure, say "I'm frightening."

*Neville:*  I'm frightening. When I have my power I'm frightening.

*Fritz:*  Say, "I frighten you with my power."

*Neville:*  I frighten you with my power.

*Fritz:*  Where do you feel power? In your hands, in your muscles, where else.

*Neville:*  My eyes.

*Fritz:*  Eyes. Let's try. Close your eyes. Let's try on for size your mother.

*Neville:*  Let's try.

*Fritz:*  Your mother for size. Be a demon with her.

*Neville:*  I'm—I am your demon. I would like to take you and kill you and crush you to smitherines. I'm going to choke you till you're dead like you choked me. (Sobs) I'm gonna choke you.

*Fritz:*  Okay. Take a rest.

*Neville:*  I'm gonna choke you. You fucking bitch. (Sobs) I'll get you.

*Fritz:*  Better take the eyes.

*Neville:*  Ugh.

*Fritz:*  I would like you to switch over to a different form of fantasy. I want you to imagine a nipple and take this nipple between your teeth and crush it and grind it and squeeze it. In fantasy, I mean. Good thing she isn't here. (Chuckles) Just with your teeth. No hands. No eyes. Just teeth.

*Neville:*  (Chokes) Ugh.

*Fritz:*  Grind it down.

*Neville:*  Ugh.

*Fritz:*  Chew hard.

*Neville:*  Ugh. Ugh. Ugh.

*Fritz:*  How does it taste?

*Neville:*  Ugh. Awful. Ugh.

*Fritz:*  Say it again.

*Neville:*  Ugh.

*Fritz:* And again.

*Neville:* Ugh.

*Fritz:* Say ugh to your mother now.

*Neville:* Ugh. Ugh. Ugh. Ugh. I—I feel a little nauseated.

*Fritz:* How do you make me feel? (Pause) How do you make me feel?

*Neville:* Now you make me puke. You make me puke. You make me vomit. You make me vomit.

*Fritz:* That's enough. Close your eyes again. Your mother's in your stomach now.

*Neville:* (Coughs).

*Fritz:* She's asleep. Do you hope she sits in your stomach?

*Neville:* Keep her out of the way. (Coughs. Pause) You're in my stomach. You're in my way. I don't want you to be my food. You're in my way. Get out of there. Get the hell out of there. Ugh. (pause) I—I—I—I—I can't get any further with that. I can't feel it move.

*Fritz:* Good. Good. Now let's play a completely different fantasy. Imagine you are your mother and you're pregnant with Neville.

*Neville:* Oh, fuck.

*Fritz:* He's a monster.

*Neville:* Oh Jesus, another one and I have four already. What the hell do I need with another one? I'm going to try and get rid of him. I don't want him. There's enough. Lousy, rotten kids and I don't need a fifth one. I'm gonna get rid of him. But, I'm only going to try. I'm not going to go all the way. I'll take some medicine and if it doesn't work, well, then, I'll be stuck with him. (Pause) Oh, shit. What do I need him here for? I don't like my lousy husband anyway. What do I need another kid with him for? Seduced me into this. Ugh. Ugh. No. There's nothing much I can do about it. He's stuck. I'm stuck with it. (pauses)

*Fritz:* How do you feel?

*Neville:* I'm less tense. I'm not terrified any more.

*Fritz:* No, No, that's amazing. You're out of your trance now. See how much you are in touch now.

*Neville:* Jane—I—(laughs) Stuart, you, you're looking

right through me; you're looking at me. Virginia, I see lots of sympathy in your face. Phillip, I see sympathy in your face, too. Jimmy I see pride in your face. Frank.

*Fritz:* Well, I'm glad we know now the whole story, we also know now what's going on in the intermediate zone. We came to eliminate one piece of your mind—to give you back that power that's invested in the demon.

*Neville:* Yeah, I want that. You sure been hurting me. (pause) Nothing will hurt you. (Pause). I feel my heart beating.

## The Impasse

### A Commitment to Boredom*

*Fritz:* I'd like to have somebody without dreams, now. (to Marty) You don't dream?

*Marty:* I do dream, but I can't remember them.

*Fritz:* Okay. Take a seat. And have an encounter with your dreams. Start out: "Dreams, I don't remember you."

*Marty:* Dreams, I don't remember you.

*Fritz:* Change seats. Now you are the not remembered dreams.

*Marty:* Not remembered dreams, why don't you remember me? Sometimes I feel you could remember me if you tried a little harder, because you do dream. I could remember you if I had a paper and pencil to write you down.

*Fritz:* What are you blocking right now?

*Marty:* I think there are like small flashes of dreams, but I can't form a picture. I have small flashes of dreams, small pictures.

*Fritz:* What are you blocking now? Let's come to the following agreement. We worked yesterday with coping-withdrawing and, if you can't cope with the situation, I suggest that you withdraw to a point where you get some support. Just withdraw. There will be something happening

* Media—Psych Corporation

in the withdrawal stage. So, can you do the shuttling also when you find and encounter? Try to remember a dream or something like this. I don't know what you're doing. Withdraw, either into yourself, or go away and then come back to the dreams. See what happens then.

*Marty:* Some—something about a Safeway—a Safeway meat market, a grocery store, a supermarket, and all of a sudden it changes, and I can't remember where it changes to, but it's complete—it's a real big change, but it doesn't register at the time that it's a change, It's not anything relevant to a meat market, to a grocery store at all.

*Fritz:* Be the meat market—grocery store. What's your name?

*Marty:* Marty.

*Fritz:* Marty. So, the grocery, supermarket, whatever it is, talks, and Marty has an encounter.

*Marty:* I'm—I'm a Safeway, super grocery store, supermarket. I sell people food that they want, Sometimes I find that they get annoyed because they don't have what I want; I don't have what they want.

*Fritz:* Now, be the people.

*Marty:* What kind of an organization are you running here that you don't keep food, you don't keep things in stock that should be in stock?

*Marty:* Changes—How can I be responsible for that? People buy out all I have of something and there's no more. Changes again—It just doesn't seem to be getting anywhere.

*Fritz:* I know. Now, I want to hear an example that the person's not ready to work on a dream. You find it very often, people who do not want to face the existential dilemma. In that case, one has to do some preliminary work. Now will you do me a favor? Either shit or get off the pot. What happened? I asked you for a favor.

*Marty:* My mind was just a blank. I'm just, I'm perfectly willing to try, but if I can't, I'm just wasting your time sitting there telling you about that supermarket because that's nothing. And I just can't, it's not that I'm not willing to try. I am. It's just that I can't get anywhere with that.

*Fritz:* Come back. Now, if this is not a clear case of avoidance and skirting the issue, I don't know what is. So, you just say something to me. I give you a present. A personalized Fritz. Put me in that chair and tell him what you just told me.

*Marty:*   I'm wasting your time, Fritz.

*Fritz:*   Play Fritz.

*Marty:*   Yes, you are. What is it that you're trying to avoid? Changes; I don't know. You told me to shit or get off the pot. That kind of scared me, Fritz. It made my mind sort of close up even more to (pause) now the harder I try, the more the blank is.

*Fritz:*   Yah. We have a very good example here of the impasse. You notice how he's stuck. Blotting out what's going on. Making himself blind; a cover. We had this impasse already, a little bit, when we spoke about marriages, didn't we? I don't remember if we had it in this group. Do you feel that you're at an impasse?

*Marty:*   Yes, I do.

*Fritz:*   Now this is the phenomenon, this is what is obvious. So, can you tell us your experience in being stuck?

*Marty:*   It's frustration. There's tension. But it's still a blank. I don't even know what I'm supposed to be hiding. Because what I've said hasn't made any sense to me or given me any idea of anything relevant to me, or, I don't—I just don't know.

*Fritz:*   Yah. Now, are you aware of the repeating sentence as compulsive repetition? You're repeating the sentence, I don't know. So let's work from there. It came out first when you said, what are you hiding? You said I don't know. You're hiding I don't know. So let's work from there. Take this seat again. And this person in the seat, says Marty, you should know.

*Marty:*   Marty, you should know. (Pause) I know I should know. It just doesn't make any sense. There's even more a feeling of confusion, now.

*Fritz:*   Yah. Describe this experience.

*Marty:*   It's—everything's just tumbling around.

*Fritz:*   Yah.

*Marty:*   I'm trying to grab something, anywhere, and I—

*Fritz:*   I notice that you're trying to grab with your right hand. Now, grab with your left hand. (pause—telephone ringing in background).

*Marty:* I notice that the instant that that telephone started ringing I just, I grabbed right onto it.

*Fritz:* Yah. Talk to the telephone.

*Marty:* Telephone, why are you ringing?

*Fritz:* Well, I don't think you are telling the truth. My impression was you grabbed on to the disturbance so you could withdraw from me, from the situation, to the telephone. Right? So talk to the telephone ring as your savior.

*Marty:* Tele—Telephone ring, I'm, (Cough) I'm grabbing onto you to remove me from, from an embarrassing situation.

*Fritz:* Ah! You feel embarrassed.

*Marty:* Not, not really embarrassed—it doesn't make any sense.

*Fritz:* So close your eyes. Now go away from this, this horrible situation here. (Pause) Just get lost. And come back to us. Where were you?

*Marty:* I was fishing.

*Fritz:* Yah.

*Marty:* At, (sigh) a place in the mountains, in California, that I really like.

*Fritz:* Good. Close your eyes again. Go back to that place and tell us what you're doing there.

*Marty:* I'm—I'm standing on, on top of some rocks and, and I'm sitting on a rock, in the middle of the river, in some rapids, watching the water go by. (cough) and I'm afraid, I'm afraid of falling in the water. But that—that doesn't make any sense, either, because I wasn't afraid of falling in the water when I was there.

*Fritz:* So, come back to us here. How do you experience being here?

*Marty:* The colors are bright. Everyone's looking at me very intensely; expectantly.

*Fritz:* Now go away again. Go back to your fishes, and I suggest, fall into the water. See what happens. Hmmm? What happens now?

*Marty:* No, nothing, I just fell in the water.

*Fritz:* And?

*Marty:* I just ended up in a—a pool. And just came to the side of the pool and got out.

*Fritz:* So come back to us. Did you come back to us?

*Marty:* (Sighing)

*Fritz:* No. Now look at me. How do you experience me?

*Marty:* As—as a wise old man with a beard.

*Fritz:* What do you resent about me?

*Marty:* I sense a—a cold something; something a little cold in you somewhere.

*Fritz:* Can you see me as the supermarket that doesn't give you what you want?

*Marty:* Yeah. Kind of.

*Fritz:* So, say once more what you resent in me.

*Marty:* I—I resent that you're sometimes impersonal, or appear to be impersonal.

*Fritz:* And, every resentment has demand behind it. So tell me what's the demand behind your resentment? What should I be like?

*Marty:* It—it doesn't seem fair, to me, to ask you to be more personal, because you are you.

*Fritz:* Okay, well it's not fair here. Put the ideal Fritz there, and play him how he should be. Let the ideal Fritz talk to Marty. (Coughing) No, be the Fritz and give Marty whatever he wants.

*Marty:* Hello, Marty. I'm pleased to meet you.

*Fritz:* All right, do this with each member of the group. Play Fritz. Be Fritz with each member of the group. Get up and go around.

*Marty:* Hello, Uh, now, (sighing).

*Fritz:* Yah, Yah, Yah.

*Marty:* It seems, it just seems so damn stupid. I—I—I—it'd be like a tape recorder. Hello, hello, hello, hello.

*Fritz:* Play this tape recorder, hello, hello, hello. Play it and make it, make a caricature or comedy out of it.

*Marty:* Hello. (Laughter) hello, Hi, Hello. Hi. How are you? How are you? Hello. Hello. Hi. Hello. Hello. (Laughter)

*Fritz:* And, what about me? You're still shaking your head.

*Marty:* It's not so easy. I just, I—

*Fritz:*   You didn't say hello to me.
*Marty:*   Hello, Fritz.
*Fritz:*   Do you mean that?
*Marty:*   No, I don't (Laughter).
*Fritz:*   Try once more.
*Marty:*   Hello, Fritz.
*Fritz:*   Mean it?
*Marty:*   I mean it.

## Self-Sabotage*

(Abe, a psychiatrist in his mid-forties, is a participant in a month-long workshop. His work with Dr. Perls is in an advanced stage and the impasses that Abe reaches are complex and not easily resolved. At this session's start, Abe is relaxed but eager to work.)

*Fritz:* (voice over) We often wonder that very little happens when people go to psycho-therapy for years, decades, and centuries. They've proven and proven and proven that nothing really changes or happens, and we take it for granted that little changes are only welcome. Actually, nobody really considered this sad fact, and yet the Russians saw this in a slightly different way. They say in the center of every neurosis is a sick point and they say the sick point cannot be overcome. So they resign themselves to that fact and organize their energies around the sick point.

I see the situation differently. I see the sick point as a kind of an impasse; as a place where people are stuck, whether they are stuck in their marriage, whether they are stuck in their therapy, whether they are stuck in their inner-conflict, all the patient desires is to maintain the status quo. At best, it cheats therapists, it cheats the contents of the inner conflict, they get a divorce and get in the same trouble again, but the basic impasse remains.

Now, in the following film we see Abe in an impasse, and not a simple impasse. He really is stuck with himself.

*Media—Psych Corporation

You see how this inner-conflict between his "top-dog" or super-ego and his "under-dog" or intra-ego, how these two parts are fighting and how they frustrate each other, how they torture each other, how they pull the rank from under each other, all in a very subtle way, slightly, seemingly cooperative, but always sabotaging and self-defeating. We don't see at any moment that Abe is getting out of this impasse. So the dynamic of the impasse, the ability to retain this status-quo and not getting to the authentic personality is very well illustrated in contrast to the other impasse situation. You see the impasse dissolving into explosions and from there, getting to the authentic person.

*Abe:* (In the hot seat) I don't do anything about it, I wait and I hope. I read without comprehending—several times while I've been here the hole has gone away and I've turned on for about a half a day.

*Fritz:* (He begins to sing in German) Can you sing it?

*Abe:* (Singing the same song) Not sure of the words. (Dr. Fritz and Abe sing the song together with Abe finishing alone.)

*Fritz:* Go into the grave.

*Abe:* I'm in the grave now. It's peaceful and quiet, nobody bothers me. I get bothered by my own voices which say "You shouldn't be lying here peaceful and quiet, you should be doing something, you should have contacts.

*Fritz:* Okay, this is the top dog. Can you show us?

*Abe:* (Moves to a chair placed in front of him as top dog) What are you doing lying here in the grave, dead before your time? You shouldn't be enjoying this peacefulness and this deadness. Get off your ass! Do something, no matter what it is; do something. You just lie there. (He moves back to the hot seat as the under dog) Screw you! I don't want to do anything. That's what I want to do right now. I want to lie here. I've been torturing myself for a long time. I know what has pleased me. But right now I don't know what pleases me. Lying around and taking it easy does please me. Staying away does please me. After I've stayed away I can come out, make some contact with people, and that sure pleases me. I don't stay there very long and I go away again, *that* pleases me and I don't like your voice saying "Stay around longer Abe, its just been a short visit" Boy, my mouth is dry. . .

*Fritz:* I'm more interested to find out what are your needs and what are his needs. You realize the best support you can get is from your inner own needs and not from external commands. So let's find out what are your needs and what are his needs.

*Abe:* (He moves to the other chair) I know that my needs are for interaction with people. I'm not sure how I sabotage those needs.

*Fritz:* Okay, I'd like now to play back the story to get more clarification about you and your dead father. Play this, you and your dead father.

*Abe:* All my mind goes back to is something that happened to us several years before your death. At least once we were able to talk to each other openly and with feeling. You said you were proud of me. I said I loved you . . . Even then I had to choke back my tears, I could only let myself have some of the tears. But how nice it was for me to put my arms around you and to have this expression of feeling between us and I'm so glad that at least once before your death we were able to have this. (He moves to the hot seat as his father) That was important to me too, Abe. I had much more feeling for you than I could say. I don't know if you knew that. But I think you do know how much trouble I've had expressing my feelings. Thank you, Abe, now I have things to say to you. How good it is for me to hear you say these things. How much I appreciate you saying these things to me because I've been afraid because of my distance. How was I to know what your feelings were? There have been so many times when you haven't written or so many times when we haven't been in touch, so I haven't been sure of your love, and I haven't been sure of the love of the other children.

*Fritz:* Now I'm going to change the scene again. I want the same kind of replay between your top dog and under dog. I want the top dog not to appreciate Abe.

*Abe:* (moves to the chair as top dog) Even though I'm a bully, I do appreciate you, Abe. But, I can't find my appreciation right now.

*Fritz:* Can you start now: "Abe, there's nothing in you to be appreciated."

*Abe:* I don't really feel that.

*Fritz:* Oh?

*Abe:* Abe, I haven't yet found—I haven't found at this moment what there is to appreciate in you. I appreciate that there's a lot more in you than you show. I appreciate that there's a great deal of love in you that sometimes you need to hide. I appreciate that sometimes the playfulness and the delight and the fun do come out and they can be delightful. I appreciate that you are interested and concerned.

*Fritz:* You know, I see part of your work as if any moment you're ready to make a joke out of it.

*Abe:* Well, there are times when I'm aware of censoring of jokes but I don't think I'm doing that now. No, I don't feel close to joke-making right now. In fact, I feel kind of heavy with my seriousness.

*Fritz:* Say this to the room.

*Abe:* (he moves back into the hot seat) I feel heavy with my seriousness, I project impatience onto you. But as I look at you I don't see that at all; I see a great deal of interested concern. There are a number of faces in which I don't see it and that feels okay too, because I *do* see it in many faces.

*Fritz:* I don't see it in any faces.

*Abe:* Your face looks softer to me now, Jenny, than I have ever seen it and I really like it that way, I like *you* that way. I haven't been able to believe or find much softness in you.

*Fritz:* So get back to your own feeling of deadness or aliveness, whatever it is.

*Abe:* I was mystified and frightened. I've calmed down a lot. Now I find some kind of vibrations going through my torso.

*Fritz:* Can you go back and find not much in us?

*Abe:* Yeah, immediately I found much in Stewart and not so much in Tommy and Dianna seemed to be far away and so I found not much.

*Fritz:* So withdraw again and see what you find in yourself again.

*Abe:* (pounding his feet on the floor) Wake up! Feet are

certainly awake. Can't sleep that way. At this moment I feel that I've lost many people. If I play to the group I say, "that was phony movement," but my answer is "fuck you, that was not phony movement, that's what I wanted to do and I did it." Fritz says "To whom are you talking?" I was talking to the group. Everybody wake up! And, top dog, for you I have a surprising fate—just wondering how to overcome with a slow and painful death. Now, top dog, is there something you'd like me to do, anything you'd like me to do? Go ahead, I'm putty in your hands, take over. (he moves to the chair as top dog) Yeah, there's a lot of things I've got for you. For one thing, liven up, waken up this crew, entertain them, unpoison them, bring them back to life. (he moves to the hot seat as under dog) Top dog, for you I'd do anything (he snores, pretending to be asleep) I'm sorry, did you say something? Oh, yeah. Okay. (pretends to be asleep again). What's the matter top dog? You're not doing so hot. You've gotten a little smaller. Something else you'd like me to do? You know you've got a lot of assignments, you've always got a lot of assignments. Take out the list and read afew. Now, who's being top dog? (he moves to the chair as top dog) Okay Abe, talk in a warm, natural voice that reaches people. Now you're getting it. (he again moves to the hot seat as under dog) Okay, top dog, anything for you. I'm going to say interesting, lively things in a vibrant and warm voice. Now listen to me carefully because you don't want to miss any of the details. That's enough of this game. You're only partially poisoned, you're just wilting a little bit, I haven't hit you very hard yet. Let's get with it now. (moving to the chair he resumes as top dog) You ought to be able to be ingenious and inventive and knock me out with one blow. You ought to be creative and draw on your own resources. It's terrible if you don't and if you're bright and original and really kill me and poison me good, then everybody will laugh and they'll be delighted and they'll have a lot of fun and they'll love you, Abe. Maybe they'll take you back into the club. I'm a much better poisoner than you are, Abe. I've been at it a much longer time. I've got experience in ways of poisoning that you couldn't begin to reach. For instance, just give you a little one, you know I can fill you chock full of poison by just reminding you that Stewart and Jane are asleep; they're bored. See, look, you've wilted already. You're not much of an antagonist. You're poisoned already, aren't you? (he moves to the hot seat) Yeah, I'm not doing so hot. Stewart and Jane shouldn't be asleep.

*Fritz:* Now poison them for their crime.

*Abe:* You shouldn't be asleep Stewart and Jane. I'm going to poison you for being asleep . . . I don't have to. You look poisoned. I'm poisoning you right now. I've gone back to poisoning me.

## The Impasse of Tony

(Tony a young man, is sitting in the chair next to Dr. Perls. Neither of them speaks for several minutes. Finally Dr. Perls calls to another member of the group.)

*Fritz:* Dick, didn't you tell me Tony wanted to work on a dream?

*Tony:* (Haltingly) I recently had a dream in which—I had an opportunity to go abroad. I've never been out of New York. I'd never been to Europe. And I had an opportunity to go to Europe and I was going to fly from New York but I had to get a flight from my home in Ohio.

*Fritz:* Please tell it in the present tense.

*Tony:* Okay, I've got to go to New York.

*Fritz:* What's your left foot doing?

*Tony:* Bracing against that little stool.

*Fritz:* Close your eyes and enter your body. Describe what you feel physically.

*Tony:* Fear. Physically, I'm warm. I'm breathing hard and my heart is pounding.

*Fritz:* What kind of voice do you use?

*Tony:* It's more sure than it actually is. It's affected.

*Fritz:* Well, you see it is clear that he is much too preoccupied with the stage fright to be ready to really work on the dream. We'll do some actual work first. Now, can you look at the audience? What do you experience there?

*Tony:* (Silently looking around the room) I—feel better. I experience—sort of a patience and I think they have a—

*Fritz:* Close your eyes and withdraw again. Any place you would like to go? Where would you go?

*Tony:* Do you mean in my body?

*Fritz:* Where you would feel more comfortable, away from us; your body, your fantasy, I don't know, just go away.

*Tony:* I'm out on one of the rocks out in the ocean.

*Fritz:* Yeah, what are you doing there?

*Tony:* I'm looking back at Esalen, at the grounds.

*Fritz:* Yeah, are you all by yourself there?

*Tony:* Yeah.

*Fritz:* How does it feel to·be by yourself?

*Tony:* Well, I feel secure in the fact that I'm out here. And yet I feel incomplete in that I should be back on the grounds, encountering people.

*Perls:* Okay, open your eyes and encounter people.

*Tony:* (He pauses for a long time as he looks at the members of the group.)

*Fritz:* What do you experience?

*Tony:* Again I experience a patience and sort of a calm, and uh—a good feeling—a rapport.

*Fritz:* A good feeling. I see your right hand doing this. (Tony's right hand is clutching his right knee.) What does this mean? How do you experience this?

*Tony:* As tension.

*Fritz:* What kind of tension? May I interpret it? May I make a mistake? It looks to me like pushing away. Okay, now close your eyes again and withdraw into your dream. What do you see, feel, and hear? I don't want a story, I just want to see what you encounter when you go into your dream.

*Tony:* Shame.

*Fritz:* Yeah, what are you ashamed of?

*Tony:* Of not accomplishing—trivial little things.

*Fritz:* Such as.

*Tony:* I-uh—I wasted just enough time so that I missed the airplane, and the opportunity to go to Europe. I—

*Fritz:* Have you ever been to Europe?

*Tony:* No.

*Fritz:* Keep your eyes closed. Go to Europe, whatever

Europe means to you. Go to Europe. What happens? Take the plane. I don't let you miss the plane. I put you on the plane.

*Tony:* Uh, Uh—new people. A lot of people I don't know and they don't know me—uh, fresh personalities that—I mean that—they're all in need.

*Fritz:* For this you have to go to Europe?

*Tony:* (Sighing) I don't know if that's my exact motivation—that's what I'm seeing when I get there. That's one of the first things I experience.

*Fritz:* Okay, now I put you back on the plane again. The plane lands in Monterey and I put you on a helicopter down to Esalen. You walk up to Fritz's room and open your eyes and what happens here? Open your eyes.

*Tony:* (Pausing for several minutes) I want to ask you what it is that you would imagine that I would do. I'm not—sort of what you would expect.

*Fritz:* Okay, produce a few expectations.

*Tony:* Sir?

*Fritz:* Produce a few expectations. (Tony sits in Dr. Perls' "empty chair" and they sit in silence for several minutes. Please don't change your posture. What are your right hand and left hand doing? How are they relating to each other?

*Tony:* (Tony is pounding his right fist into his cupped left hand.) It's an encounter—tension.

*Fritz:* Can you sit here and keep the posture? (Dr. Perls motions for Tony to return to his seat which he does and cups his right hand in his left). What does the right hand say and what does the left hand say?

*Tony:* The left hand is stopping the right hand from moving—but the right hand has a grip, or has a catch—is holding the left hand.

*Fritz:* Give them words. "I stop you." "I hold on to you." Make a Punch and Judy show out of it. Make it like two puppets talking to each other.

*Tony:* The left hand is saying, "Stop."

*Fritz:* Say it again.

*Tony:* Stop!

*Fritz:* Again.

*Tony:* Stop!
*Fritz:* Louder.
*Tony:* Stop!
*Fritz:* Louder.
*Tony:* Stop!
*Fritz:* Louder.
*Tony:* Stop!
*Fritz:* What does the right hand say?
*Tony:* (He sits silently for several seconds) The right hand isn't going anywhere but it doesn't care because—
*Fritz:* Now, say I don't care.
*Tony:* I don't care.
*Fritz:* Again.
*Tony:* I don't care.
*Fritz:* Again.
*Tony:* I don't care.
*Fritz:* Again.
*Tony:* I don't care.
*Fritz:* Okay, now go into the dialogue.
*Tony:* You must stop pushing. No, I don't: Stop pushing immediately!

(The film pauses at this moment to allow the camera to be reloaded. During this period, Tony completes the dialogue between the left and right hands, a conversation that ends in an impasse. Dr. Perls directs Tony's attention to the group. The film resumes.)

*Tony:* (Tony surveys the group quietly.) It isn't a fear, but I sense that other people are—sort of gaining an insight—possibly to me.
*Fritz:* Other people gain insight, but you don't. It's still there—other people.
*Tony:* Yeah. I'm starting to formulate something.
*Fritz:* I know, but don't force yourself. Well, there is one thing that I want to point out that you might have noticed. Tony is an example of the implosive layer. There's an implosion here. (Fritz illustrates this layer by re-enacting Tony's hand dialogue.) He is paralyzing himself—both sides are exerting equal pressure so the result is like a tug of war with no side winning. This is how he keeps himself in this fit of near-paralysis. He has to separate the parts and let them

mobilize themselves separately. (Turning to Tony and shaking hands) Okay?

## Resurrection—Dick*

*Fritz:* (voice over) We are really spoiled in Gestalt therapy. We are so used to having dramatic happenings, so used to having break-throughs. Means of self-expression occur sometimes in half an hour. So we also have to consider another possibility: that some development might take weeks, even, in the following case, a month. In other words, we don't always deliver instant cure.

Dick has been at a four week workshop. He comes in as a corspe, really *imploded,* rigid, not much chance of getting him going, getting him moving. But you see development —from week to week. You see him now in the first week.

(Dick is thirty-six. He sits next to Dr. Perls and is crying in anguish. His sobs are interrupted only by heavy and labored gasps for air.)

*Dick:* I'm back under control.

*Fritz:* So let's do the opposite. So say to Tony, "Mistake is a different way of doing things."

*Dick:* Tony, mistake is a different way of doing things. Neville, mistake is a different way of doing things. Now I'm the computer.

*Fritz:* Try to say—

*Dick:* It hurts. It presses me down.

*Fritz:* How?

*Dick:* Right here, right here in my chest.

*Fritz:* How?

*Dick:* It feels heavy.

*Fritz:* Is it soft? (Dick pushes Fritz' chest) You don't bother me, you do it with me.

*Dick:* Pushes you in.

*Fritz:* I push you in.

*Dick:* I push you in.

*Fritz:* More.

* Media—Psych Corporation

*Dick:*   Heavily. I hang heavy.

*Fritz:*   More.

*Dick:*   On your chest—real heavy.

*Fritz:*   More.

*Dick:*   Impose on you. I feel heavy on you. I make you hold in. I don't know what I'm doing.

*Fritz:*   You make me breathe better. (laughter)

*Fritz:*   (voice over) After the first, we enter now the second week. Begin to say "I don't want to blame you."

*Dick:*   I don't want to blame you.

*Fritz:*   Again.

*Dick:*   I don't want to blame you.

*Fritz:*   Louder.

*Dick:*   *I don't want to blame you.*

*Fritz:*   Again.

*Dick:*   I don't want to blame you (crying) I want to blame you. (softly) I want to blame you. I feel helpless with you. I can't deal with you like I've had to deal with you.

*Fritz:*   Let's try the sentence "I always try to do the right thing."

*Dick:*   I always try to do the right thing. I always try to do the right thing.

*Fritz:*   Can you talk to them about mistakes? How do you deal with mistakes?

*Dick:*   I was a mistake. You were a mistake. Everything I do you take for granted.

*Fritz:*   (voice over) Now we have the third week . . . (Dick is on the floor in front of the 'hot seat' and is pounding with his fists.)

*Dick:*   I feel my heart beating. I don't want to go back to another damn bitch. I see the beginning of it in my mother. I think we are associated with some of the same things now. All I know is I—

*Fritz:*   Dick, do you see me?

*Dick:*   I see you.

*Fritz:*   So go back into yourself again. (Dick continues to pound on the floor.)

*Fritz:*   How old are you now?

*Dick:*   Fourteen is the first thing that hits my mind.

*Fritz:*   And the real age?

*Dick:* Thirty-six.

*Fritz:* Thirty-six. Can you for a moment try to be thirty-six? Be your age and consider the possibility of coping with that woman called mother. Try the rationale of the computer approach for a moment.

*Dick:* Why are you just another woman? You just happened to be the one who had me. It's just an accident of life and now I am—now I'm out and I'm gone. I barely knew you. When I was struggling back here I felt like I was Atlas for a moment—my hands were up and so much anger and holding the fucking world on my back. And I take responsibility—I take responsibility for her. I take responsibility for you . . . I take responsibility for you and Dad . . . I haven't wanted it.

*Fritz:* What's the purpose? Does it make you feel noble?

*Dick:* It makes me feel guilty.

*Fritz:* If you take the responsibility it makes you feel guilty?

*Dick:* No, no, I take the responsibility because I feel guilty. I resent you for not being what *I* needed.

*Fritz:* Now you're starting to make sense. Could you use my sentence—you didn't live up to my expectations.

*Dick:* You didn't live up to my expectations. *You* didn't live up to my expectations.

*Fritz:* And I'll never forgive you for that.

*Dick:* And I'll never forgive you for that—I've *never* forgiven you for that. I resent you for having me the way you did. You wouldn't take the responsibility for *me.* I won't take the responsibility for you.

*Fritz:* (voice over) And finally, finally we come to the Resurrection . . . the explosion, the bursting in two.

(In a final session, Dick becomes aware of the group's support and experiences an explosion into joy. He rises from Dr. Perls' 'hot seat' and, laughing-crying, hugs each member in the workshop.)

*Fritz:* (voice over) If you consider how long it took to get Dick moving, then you can appreciate the tremendous impact it had on him and the group, when he finally burst out into joy. Outbursts into self-pity, anger, even grief are not rare in therapy. But the real joy is not easily found. There is not such a thing as dispensing instant cure or instant sensory awareness. It has to be worked through and real meaning has to be acquired.

### Resurrection—Nancy

(Nancy is sitting in the hot seat, next to Dr. Perls. She is a young woman of about thirty, extremely emaciated, with a childlike face.)

*Nancy:*   I feel very frightened.

*Fritz:*   How? Give us the details of your experience. The simplest way to get to the how is to inquire about details. Then, automatically, if you do, some development begins to take place.

*Nancy:*   I feel very hot in my face. I feel burning under my arms. My hands feel very cold. And my voice is very shaky. I feel the coldness in my toes. I feel a burning here in my arm.

*Fritz:*   What?

*Nancy:*   Burning here in my arm. My throat is very dry. I swallowed. (Pause) I feel my legs on the chair.

*Fritz:*   You're looking at me. What do your eyes say?

*Nancy:*   Help me.

*Fritz:*   Louder.

*Nancy:*   Help me.

*Fritz:*   Louder.

*Nancy:*   Help me!

*Fritz:*   Scream it.

*Nancy:*   (Screaming) *Help me!–*

*Fritz:*   Scream it!

*Nancy:*   (Screaming louder) HELP ME! (She is crying.) (Long pause; Fritz smokes)

*Fritz:*   What do your eyes say now?

*Nancy:*   Help me.

*Fritz:*   How? With what?

*Nancy:*   With anything you have.

*Fritz:*   What kind of help do you need?

(Long pause)

*Nancy:*   I want you to tell me something. (Pause) I want you to like me.

*Fritz:* Say this again.

*Nancy:* I want you to like me.

*Fritz:* Do you like me?

*Nancy:* Yes.

*Fritz:* What do you like about me?

*Nancy:* I like your eyes, and I like your kindness.

*Fritz:* Can you tell each one of us in one or two sentences what you like about each one of us?

*Nancy:* (Going around room, speaking to each person) I like your frown. And I like your softness. And Paul, I admire you because you're here. And Barbara, I like how I felt when you talked about your husband and I like you when you play with the kitten. And Dick, I like you when you're soft. And Page, I like you because I feel you're a real person.

*Fritz:* Now put Nancy in that chair and tell her what you like about her.

*Nancy:* (Pause) It's hard to think of things I like about you.

*Fritz:* What?

*Nancy:* I said, it's hard to think of things I like about me.

*Fritz:* You're lying.

*Nancy:* (Pause, then, to herself) I like you because you're sensitive to people.

*Fritz:* Go on.

*Nancy:* (Pause) And you can see into them. (Pause) And you can listen to them.

*Fritz:* What else? (Long pause) Come on, don't be so mean.

*Nancy:* (Laughing and gripping chair.) I like you because you're intelligent. I like you better because you are warm to people—

*Fritz:* Now change seats: "Oh, that's nothing—"

*Nancy:* Change seats?

*Fritz:* Talk back to her. You just gave you some appreciation, now deprecate what you got. (Nancy changes chairs.)

*Nancy:* It's nothing; a lot of people are intelligent.

*Fritz:* Yes, go on. Sneer at her.

*Nancy:* (Sarcastic voice) So what? Big deal. (Pause) So you can see into other people, you're warm . . . (mumbles, shakes head Long pause) Couldn't think of very much else to say. (Pause.)

*Fritz:* Change seats.

*Nancy:* (Changes back to hot seat) Maybe if you'd look a little deeper.

*Fritz:* Now let's go to the opposite. Tell her what you dislike about her.

*Nancy:* (sniffs, blows nose) The sneerer?

*Fritz:* Huh?

*Nancy:* The sneerer? What I dislike about her?

*Fritz:* Yah. Call her the sneerer, and so on. What do you dislike about Nancy?

*Nancy:* (Slowly) I dislike your thinness. I dislike your thinking all the time. I dislike your numbness and your tenseness. (She sits very still; pauses)

*Fritz:* Can you give me a straight answer if I ask you a question? Without thinking? The first thing that comes up, yah? When did you die?

*Nancy:* (Instantly) Now! (She cries) I feel—your hand. (sobbing, she takes Fritz's hand, touches it to her face. Then she looks at Fritz, touches his knee, gets up and hugs him.)

*Fritz:* Would you do something for me, Nancy? Get up and dance.

(Nancy gets up and dances around the circle, open and free.)

*Fritz:* Can you sing anything with the dancing?

*Nancy:* (laughing and crying and dancing) I have an awful voice! Yeah! Yeah! (There is general laughter, Nancy dances around in the circle and sings, finally falling in a heap into Fritz' lap.)

*Fritz:* Feel a bit of life?

*Nancy:* (Sniffling) Yes. (She sits down in her chair, smiles around the room.)

*Fritz:* Let go. Let go! Do whatever you want to do! (General laughter.)

(Nancy goes to each person in the room, hugging and kissing him, shaking his hand, looking at each one quietly, giving bear hugs, joyous and laughing, with a lot of confused comments and exchanges.)

*Fritz:* This is what is commonly known as the resurrection. (Nancy, sitting down now, touches her hand to her face.)

## Explosions

### Evelyn

(Evelyn, a heavy blond woman of about fifty, is sitting next to Fritz. Fritz is talking to her.)

*Fritz:* I want you to play your parents once more, putting the baby into the mail.

*Evelyn:* (As her Father) All right now, Betty, wrap that baby up carefully in the box. (As step-mother) Reg, are you sure Evelyn will take it? I just don't know. It just makes me nervous, thinking about it. You think she'll really take it? (As father) You know very well she will. She's always helpful and she said she'd help us in any way. She was the only one who encouraged us to go ahead and get married, and I— (As step-mother) Well, Reg, I'm just worried about sending the baby through the mail. (Evelyn, as herself) She's a very hysterical, silly woman.

*Fritz:* Talk to her.

*Evelyn:* Betty, you're a very hysterical, silly woman. But I'm glad you married my father. And I appreciate your taking care of him when he's old and not able to take care of himself. I think the rest of the family are—are silly to condemn you for marrying him. And I'd take any damn baby you had, any time, just so you'll take care of my dad. (General laughter) I love you for that. He's a bastard, and I know it. Dad— Gee, he treated everyone in the family mean, but the fact that you're willing to love him and take care of him—I think it's great, just great!

*Fritz:* Can you accept your Daddy as a baby, as your baby?

*Evelyn:* My Daddy as a—?

*Fritz:* Your father; he needs taking care of.

*Evelyn:* Dad, you'd be awfully hard to take care of. I don't think I—Oh, I'm damn sure I couldn't do it. I have too much resentment towards you—because of the way you treated my mother and all six of us.

*Fritz:* Okay, Start out "Daddy, I resent you—"

*Evenly:* Daddy, I resent your drinking so much. Daddy, I resent your beating my brothers with the hose. Daddy, I even resent your killing the chickens. Daddy, I resent your smashing the piano because you didn't like my playing it. Daddy, I resent your constant use of foul language. (Pause) But I appreciate your working and supporting the family for all those years.

*Fritz:* Go on with your appreciations.

*Evelyn:* I appreciate that you never left us when your brothers did leave their wives. I appreciate the fact that you were always around. I appreciate that you were always very proud of me, that you always had something good to say about me, and I appreciate that you—You let me run away to the woods and that you never came after me.

*Fritz:* You know, you talk to him like legalese, as if you were condemning him.

*Evelyn:* Very officious.

*Fritz:* Ya. Ya.

*Evelyn:* I feel that.

*Fritz:* You keep all emotions out.

*Evelyn:* I try to, because I want to be fair with him.

*Fritz:* Say this to him now.

*Evelyn:* I want to be fair with you, Dad. For so many years I wasn't fair with you. All I could do is condemn you, condemn you. And I know now, looking back on it, that there were so many good things about you that I couldn't see at the time. (Pause) And I don't want you to die; I want you to live.

*Fritz:* Say this again.

*Evelyn:* At one time, I used to want you to die every day of my life. I used to think the most wonderful thing that could happen to our family would be to wake up and find you dead. And yet every day, you were there. Now I'm damn glad you were. I don't know what we would have done without you.

*Fritz:* Close your eyes. Look at him. What do you see?

*Evelyn:* I see a very helpless old man.

*Fritz:* Say this to him. Still with this image.

*Evelyn:* You really weren't a bear, you were just a helpless old man; and now just a helpless old man who needs my help. You're just pathetic. And now nobody cares for you, nobody wants to help you. Nobody wants you, Daddy. No one. Because no one can forgive you for all the things you did.

*Fritz:* You try. "Dad, I forgive you for this and this and this."

*Evelyn:* Daddy, I forgive you for all those things. (She is crying) I forgive you for the swearing. I forgive you for the drunkenness. I forgive you for the cruel treatment. I forgive you for blaming me for Mother's death. (She cries and sobs. Long pause.)

*Fritz:* Can you tell him that he can now die in peace?

*Evelyn:* (Crying) You can die in peace. (Pause, Sighs.)

*Fritz:* What do you feel right now?

*Evelyn:* Relief. Tremendous relief.

*Fritz:* Could you close your eyes once more. Once more go to him. Touch him. Hold him, and tell him that you forgive him.

*Evelyn:* Oh, Daddy, I forgive you. (Sobbing) I *do*. I do forgive you. Please believe me. Please . . .

*Fritz:* Is he accepting it?

*Evelyn:* Yes. I feel that I should go get on a plane and go do this. Right away. (She is crying.)

*Fritz:* Call him up.

*Evelyn:* Hello, Dad. Dad, this is Evelyn. I've got something to tell you. It's terribly important. Please listen to me. Listen carefully, because it means so much to me, and if I could tell you this and you'd understand, it'd—it's—I know it's going to help me in a lot of my relationships. I didn't forgive you for a long time for all the things you did I felt were so wrong, and I had a lot of resentment towards you, and this resentment, I—I don't feel that way any more, and I want you to know that it's all over with and I don't resent you any more.

*Fritz:* Can you tell him, "I don't hate you any more."

*Evelyn:* I don't hate you any more. (She is crying). I don't hate you at all. I love you, Dad. I love you.

*Fritz:*   Say this again.

*Evelyn:*   I love you, Daddy. You're the only Daddy I could ever have. (Softly) I love you. (Pause) You know what he said?

*Fritz:*   What did he say?

*Evelyn:*   He said, "For God's said, I knew that." He said, "What the hell's the matter with you, Evelyn. I knew that." (Laughter)


## Bob's Two-Way Street*

(Bob, a heavy-set man of about forty, is in the hot seat. He is a psychiatrist and has done considerable work in Gestalt therapy.)

*Fritz:*   What are you doing with your mouth?

*Bob:*   Biting my lower lip.

*Fritz:*   How is this related to what you are thinking about?

*Bob:*   I was thinking about hanging on. Because so often when I love somebody, it is a hanging on to them. I've been aware of this, and that's—uh—that's kind of what I was doing with my lip.

*Fritz:*   Which is—who is the first person that comes to you when you speak about this hanging on?

*Bob:*   My wife.

*Fritz:*   Can we have an empty chair, please? (Somebody puts an empty chair in front of Bob). Now have an encounter with your wife about this hanging on.

*Bob:*   (Places his fingers carefully on knees, leans toward empty chair) Alice, I behave much of the time as though I don't need you, and it's hard for me to demonstrate physically because I—I get cautious about how much I hang on to you.

*Fritz:*   Now imagine her talking back. Change seats. She's sitting there. You play her.

*Bob:*   (Changes seats; speaks as Alice) I want you to hang on to me.

*Fritz:*   Now write your own script.

* Media—Psych Corporation

210

*Bob:* (Changes back to hot seat; speaks as Bob) I know, but I'm—my need to hang on to you gets— (Pause) I don't feel right now. I'm not getting—I don't feel easy with this.

*Fritz:* To whom are you saying this?

*Bob:* I'm saying this to me.

*Fritz:* Say this to Bob.

*Bob:* Bob, I— You — uh— You're kind of faking it along temporarily, hoping it will get real as you go along.

*Fritz:* What does Bob say?

*Bob:* Uh—You might as well do that, because that's the way it is right now, and if you stick with it, it will— It'll get real.

*Fritz:* In other words, you are jumping out of the present into the future. In other words, you are avoiding some experience. What do you experience right now?

*Bob:* A hot feeling in my chest.

*Fritz:* Just stay with that. Let this develop.

*Bob:* Well, I have this a lot; it's an aching and, uh—

*Fritz:* Now you are escaping into the past. You give me a piece of history, not your experience. So this must be an important image that you avoided.

*Bob:* I feel like somebody else is squeezing me.

*Fritz:* Uh-huh. Play the somebody else. You want me to be Bob again, and squeeze me?

*Bob:* No, This somebody else is a— I don't like. Because it smothers me; it squeezes me so that I can't breathe.

*Fritz:* Now say this to her.

*Bob:* Her?

*Fritz:* It came up in the context of your wife, so I assume it relates to her.

*Bob:* The word that comes to my mind right away is needy. And— I—Your needing me so much smothers me. I—

*Fritz:* It smothers you. Now we have here a rule in Gestalt therapy. We try to replace the it with I or you instead of this vague projection screen.

*Bob:* *You* smother me.

*Fritz:* Yah. Say this again.

*Bob:* You smother me with your squeezing. And all— And— (long pause.)

*Fritz:* Does she listen?

*Bob:* No.

*Fritz:* Can you say it so that you can communicate what you want to say?

*Bob:* What I would like to do is get angry, because that's the way I really feel about this.

*Fritz:* Now say this to her.

*Bob:* I'd like to get pissed off at you, but I can't because you'll . . . cry. (He laughs.) You don't allow me—

*Fritz:* What would she say to that?

*Bob:* You know, I could do this better if it were my mother.

*Fritz:* All right, if you want to switch over to your mother. See, all I do is to feed back whatever comes out and reinforce your experiences; try to keep you on keel, to stay with your experiences.

*Bob:* There's something about your unhappiness that smothers me.

*Fritz:* You're talking to your mother.

*Bob:* Yeah.

*Fritz:* What would she answer?

*Bob:* She'd say, well I don't know what you mean. And you know, then I'd probably give up. But—

*Fritz:* Let me introduce a possibility and find out whether it fits. This crying, could it be a put-on job, a role? A blackmail role, for instance?

*Bob:* Yes, I feel like it is.

*Fritz:* So say this to her.

*Bob:* Your constantly being so goddamn sad doesn't allow me to get angry at you. Because I get—

*Fritz:* It? You don't allow me to get angry at you.

*Bob:* You don't allow me to get angry at you.

*Fritz:* Tell her how she stops you from getting angry.

*Bob:* You stop me from getting angry by being so hurt all the time.

*Fritz:* Being so hurt?

*Bob:* Looking like you're hurt.

*Fritz:* Try this on for size: by playing hurt; by playing the tragedy queen, the gloom caster, the injured child, or whatever role you see her playing.

*Bob:* (Pause) I'll bear up. It's hard for me to play this.

*Fritz:* Can you tell her what she's doing? What she's playing. Can you be the psychiatrist for the moment, instead of the child?

*Bob:* Yeah. (He crosses his legs and arms and leans forward.)

*Fritz:* Notice the very moment I mentioned the word psychiatrist you became a closed system. You closed up. Before you were open. Now see what happens if you open up again. And talk to your mother as a psychiatrist. See whether you can do it in an open position.

*Bob:* (Uncrossing his arms and legs; speaking to the empty chair, to his mother) Your face looks as though you were constantly pinching yourself off from the world. You look as though somebody is always hurting you, and this makes me wonder how it must affect people that you deal with. It seems to me that it would be easy for them to feel, that you look this way—

*Fritz:* Show her. Show her how she looks. (he makes a pinched, sad face) What would she say if you should show this to her?

*Bob:* She'd just look like that more.

*Fritz:* Now say this to her.

*Bob:* I can't win, for Christ's sake, because everything I say to you hurts you more. Finally, you're just a—blob.

*Fritz:* Uh-huh. Say this again; you're just a blob.

*Bob:* No, it doesn't fit. You're really a— (He kicks the empty metal chair across the room with great force.) WHEW!

*Fritz:* What have you done to your poor mother? (General laughter.)

(Bob hits out at air with force, blows air out of his mouth.)

*Fritz:* You want to continue this explosion?

*Bob:* Yes. (He stands up.)

*Fritz:* Good. (He stands up and points at the chair he was sitting in which is large and overstuffed.) This is your mother. Give her a beating.

*Bob:* It's hard to do this with a false set-up like this.

*Fritz:* Well, this is a transition period of a possible

implosion to explosion.

*Bob:* Looking at chair, standing in front of it, hesitant) The longer I wait, you know—

*Fritz:* Say this to her.

*Bob:* The longer I wait, the harder it is. (He goes gingerly up to the chair, hits it, then hits and beats it with great force. He kicks it and pummels it with such force that he bounces it around. Pause. He holds one hand, feeling it, and blows out.) I think I broke my hand.

*Fritz:* Think so? (Bob faces Fritz and sighs, and shakes his head.) Say this to her: "You nearly broke my hand."

*Bob:* (Sitting down in the hot seat again) I really don't want to.

*Fritz:* Say this.

*Bob:* (Leaning back in chair, sighing, quiet) I don't even want to tell you that I broke my fucking hand on you. (Laughs, closes eyes)

*Fritz:* Can you say to her, "Look what you are doing to me."

*Bob:* Look what you're doing to me. (Pause) Look what you've done to me.

*Fritz:* Now I'd like to come back to the question of hanging on. Do you hang on to her, or does she hang on to you?

*Bob:* (Laughing) I think it's a two-way street.


## The Case of Marykay*

(Marykay is a young woman of about twenty-eight, blonde and attractive. She is sitting in the chair next to Dr. Perls, the hot seat. Opposite her is an empty chair.)

*Fritz:* The case of Marykay shows some paradoxes. I could call this a case where the person barks up the wrong tree. What is noticeable is that she apparently is fighting and hating her mother, has great difficulties with her. She seems on the surface an open, friendly person. And yet, when it comes to expressing affection and closeness, she is incapa-

* Media-Psych Corporation

ble. How the paradox is resolved is the task of the film shown in the next few minutes.

*Fritz:*  So put mama in that chair: "Mama, I resent you."

*Marykay:*  Oh, Mother, I really do resent you. (She is smiling.)

*Fritz:*  Now, are you watching your face? Were you aware that you are smiling?

*Marykay:*  I wasn't aware, but I—I think I was.

*Fritz:*  Yah. Now the expression of resentment and the smile are inconsistent. (She makes a smile again.) Again you make a face. You see? You feel your face?

*Marykay:*  Yah, yah, yah. (Pause—she becomes serious). Mother, I just resent you. Why can't you just leave me alone?

*Fritz:*  Say this again.

*Marykay:*  Why can't you just leave me alone? You know, why can't you let me be me?

*Fritz:*  Make your demands more explicit. Talk in imperatives.

*Marykay:*  Mother, just let me be me. You know, why don't you understand that I'm just me and you're you, and I'm just me. And why do you make me feel like you're—

*Fritz:*  Nya, nya, nya, nya. (She gives a little laugh.) Why, why, why—

*Marykay:*  All right, Okay. All right, all right.

*Fritz:*  Do this to you mother.

*Marykay:*  All right. Okay. Just let me be me, Mother! (She bangs down her hand.)

*Fritz:*  Do this again. Do this to your mother.

*Marykay:*  Oh, I can't hit her.

*Fritz:*  You can't hit your mother? Tell her that.

*Marykay:*  Well, I can't hit you, Mother. I can't hit you, but—you know sometimes I'd really like to hit you.

*Fritz:*  Say this again. Say this again. "Sometimes I'd like to hit you."

*Marykay:*  Sometimes—(to Fritz) I don't know whether I've ever wanted to hit her. I just know I just wanted her to leave me alone. You know, to understand and not make me feel like I'm always wrong. I don't *want* to be a should person. You know, why are my feelings wrong?

*Fritz:* Can you hear your voice? Nya, nya, nya, nya, nya, nya.

*Marykay:* No, but now that you've said it, I can.

*Fritz:* Now play your mother.

*Marykay:* (Changes seats to the other chair, playing mother.) Marykay, I just don't understand you. You know I love you. I love you so much, Marykay, but we're not alike and I'll just never understand you. (In a whining voice) I'll just never understand you. (She switches seats again; as Marykay) I know we're not alike Mother, and that's the whole point. Why can't you be you and me be me: And so we're not alike. I don't want to be like you. I don't want to be like you at all. I don't want to be like you, you're everything I don't want. (Scolding) Now why do you make me feel like I should be like you? Because I don't want to be like you.

*Fritz:* Can you hear your voice? Getting more strength now? There was much less wailing. Go on. Go on.

*Marykay:* (As mother) I do let you be you. I want you to be you. That's what I want—that's all I want for my children, is to be themselves. I want you to be—You know, I just love you, but we just don't understand each other. You have all these kooky friends. (She is crying a little.) You have such a bad temper. You have such a bad temper, I just don't—I just don't understand you. I've been such a terrible mother. I failed all you children.

*Fritz:* Mea culpa. Mea culpa.

*Marykay:* That's her. That's not me. Yeah. Sure is.

*Fritz:* Yeah. Tell her about that. (laughs.)

*Marykay:* Okay, you know, so it is your fault. I don't have to love you just because you're my mother.

*Fritz:* Say this again.

*Marykay:* You know, you earn love. It just isn't given because you had me. Anybody in the world could have had me. I don't have to love you because you had me. All I have—I have to love you because you earn my love, and because—because you let me feel that I'm a person and that my feelings are right, too.

*Fritz:* I'd like to interrupt it for a moment. Close your

eyes and see what you experience physically now. Something seems to be going on. (Marykay closes her eyes.) What do you feel?

*Marykay:* I feel—ah—just a deadness inside. Sort of an "Ah, what's the use." And yet, behind that there is—there is resentment.

*Fritz:* Now can you say the same paragraph to your mother?

*Marykay:* You make me feel dead. You make me feel like I'm just not even anything. And I know you don't mean it. I know that it's because you're afraid, and I know that if—And I know you love me. And I know that you're afraid. But why did I have to be the victim of your fear? Why did it have to turn out that I am the victim of your great needs?

*Fritz:* Change seats again. (She does so.) You notice the fighting is beginning to change to a little bit of mutual understanding.

*Marykay:* (As mother) I never meant it to be that way. All—I never meant it to be that way at all. I guess I just couldn't admit my own fears. I wanted—I *am* proud of you, I'm really proud of you, Marykay.

*Fritz:* Say this again.

*Marykay:* I'm really proud of you, you know. I show your picture (she is crying) to all the people at work. And I—(As Marykay, to Fritz) I feel so sorry for her.

*Fritz:* Can you imagine going to her and embracing her?

*Marykay:* No! (With great violence) No, I can't! I can't! I can't imagine—I can't imagine embracing—anybody. Oh—I couldn't even—I couldn't even embrace my Dad when I left. (She is crying bitterly.) You just can't—You just can't show feelings. They're not right.

*Fritz:* You're showing feelings now. (She is sobbing violently.) Come here, Marykay. (She turns toward Fritz.)

*Marykay:* (Breaking) Oh, please—Oh, please—(She takes him by the arms, facing him, sobbing) Oh—Oh, I just love you. (Facing Fritz, crying in his arms.)

*Fritz:* Do you feel better?

*Marykay:* I have to stop. I have to stop because you

always have to stop to take care of yourself. (A little calmer) Yeah, you really do have to take care of yourself. I'm doing a good job of it.

*Fritz:* You know, I miss something. I know the psychiatrist's tools are skill and Kleenex—where is the Kleenex? (They both smile. Someone hands Fritz a Kleenex, which he gives to Marykay.)